Stabilizing Eastern Syria After ISIS

JAMES A. SCHEAR, JEFFREY MARTINI, ERIC ROBINSON,
MICHELLE E. MIRO, JAMES DOBBINS

Prepared for the Office of the Secretary of Defense
Approved for public release; distribution unlimited

NATIONAL DEFENSE RESEARCH INSTITUTE

For more information on this publication, visit www.rand.org/t/RR2541

Library of Congress Cataloging-in-Publication Data is available for this publication.
ISBN: 978-1-9774-0201-1

Published by the RAND Corporation, Santa Monica, Calif.
© Copyright 2020 RAND Corporation
RAND® is a registered trademark.

Cover image: Muhammad Hamed / Reuters

Limited Print and Electronic Distribution Rights

This document and trademark(s) contained herein are protected by law. This representation of RAND intellectual property is provided for noncommercial use only. Unauthorized posting of this publication online is prohibited. Permission is given to duplicate this document for personal use only, as long as it is unaltered and complete. Permission is required from RAND to reproduce, or reuse in another form, any of its research documents for commercial use. For information on reprint and linking permissions, please visit www.rand.org/pubs/permissions.

The RAND Corporation is a research organization that develops solutions to public policy challenges to help make communities throughout the world safer and more secure, healthier and more prosperous. RAND is nonprofit, nonpartisan, and committed to the public interest.

RAND's publications do not necessarily reflect the opinions of its research clients and sponsors.

Support RAND
Make a tax-deductible charitable contribution at
www.rand.org/giving/contribute

www.rand.org

Preface

The U.S.-led international coalition to defeat the Islamic State of Iraq and Syria (ISIS) has achieved substantial progress over the past several years. In Eastern Syria, local partners supported by the United States liberated Raqqah City and, subsequently, a number of communities downstream along the Euphrates River. That said, the counter-ISIS campaign is not over. This report assesses humanitarian needs in Eastern Syria's Euphrates River Valley. It also examines how locally focused stabilization efforts might be orchestrated to help preclude the Islamic State's recapture of territory, even as Syria's larger civil conflict tragically continues unabated and is growing more complex.

This research was sponsored by the Office of the Under Secretary of Defense for Acquisition, Technology, and Logistics and conducted within the International Security and Defense Policy Center of the RAND National Security Research Division (NSRD), which operates the National Defense Research Institute (NDRI), a federally funded research and development center sponsored by the Office of the Secretary of Defense, the Joint Staff, the Unified Combatant Commands, the Navy, the Marine Corps, the defense agencies, and the defense intelligence enterprise.

For more information on the RAND International Security and Defense Policy Center, see www.rand.org/nsrd/isdp or contact the director (contact information is provided on the webpage).

Contents

Figures and Table

Figures

Table

Summary

As the Islamic State of Iraq and Syria (ISIS) has been largely cleared from its strongholds, the overarching challenge facing liberated communities in Eastern Syria's Middle Euphrates River Valley (MERV) is how best to restore their security, stability, and livelihoods. Although these communities are no longer occupied by ISIS, they are transitioning into a fraught political environment where the Kurdish-led Syrian Democratic Forces (SDF) and the Syrian government have both expanded their regional presence and where small pockets of insurgent ISIS fighters still remain.

Drawing on extensive research conducted during 2017 and 2018, this report opens with a sociocultural perspective on the MERV's human terrain, explicating long-standing divisions within and among the Valley's Sunni Arab tribes that may pose challenges to restoring broadly accepted local governance. We then assess the region's most urgent post-ISIS needs, focusing intensively on the status of its critical infrastructure—e.g., bridges, hospitals, transit facilities—as well as its natural resources, human displacement, and economic activity. While the level of infrastructure damage endured by the MERV's major cities and towns appears to be less than in other population centers once controlled by ISIS, the region's bridging, industrial sites, water treatment facilities, and oil and gas infrastructure have not been spared. Along with repairs in these domains, early recovery's highest-priority efforts should address shortfalls in water, electricity, and agricultural production. The latter would focus on providing short-term agricultural assistance—e.g., seeds, fertilizers, and affordable fuel—to help revive levels of crop production during the MERV's upcoming grow-ing seasons.

In the political sphere, this report examines how stabilization efforts might be pursued in a region where both the Syrian government and nonstate actors are filling a vacuum left by a common enemy's loss of territorial control. Even if each side chooses to begrudgingly accept the other's presence in Eastern Syria—and there are pressures on each side to do so—the pathway toward stabilization would not be easy to navigate. The five most consequential challenges would be

1. where to draw the deconfliction line
2. whether and how to organize mutually agreed flows of unarmed civilians, economic goods, and relief supplies across the Valley
3. managing water scarcity and sharing oil and gas revenues
4. attending to the needs of displaced communities and their influx back into the Valley following ISIS's departure
5. mitigating the risks of retributive violence against communities suspected of having ISIS sympathizers.

The report then analyzes the pluses and minuses of attempting to overcome these challenges via either a separated division of labor approach to stabilization (i.e., a "steer clear" approach) or a more col-laborative "interactive" template. It recommends that both sides should start with a minimalist steer clear option but incrementally move toward a more interactive approach, as conditions permit.

To facilitate a stabilization contingency, the report concludes by highlighting a series of recommended actions spanning three key areas.

First, for the MERV overall, these priorities would include orches-trating a surge of relief aid to liberated communities; managing the influx of returning refugees and internally displaced persons (IDPs); ramping up repairs to water pumping stations and the electrical grid, along with the provision of agricultural assistance; developing plans for more extensive recovery of public services; working with Turkey on Euphrates River water management over the longer term; and ensuring transparency of external support for relief aid and local infrastructure repairs.

Secondly, for areas of the MERV held by U.S.-backed coalition partners, priority actions would focus on assisting communities in removing explosive hazards, supporting the formation of locally focused civil councils, ramping up efforts to generate locally accepted Sunni Arab security forces, refining screening procedures to facilitate the returns of refugees and IDPs, repairing damaged oil and gas facilities previously held by ISIS, and countering youth radicalization through curricular reforms in the education sector.

Finally, for heightening the prospects of interactive stabilization, key recommended steps would include mapping out the MERV's socioeconomic interdependences to preview likely cross-river flows of people and economic goods, crafting protocols for processing transiting cargo and people through checkpoints, developing a plan for sharing oil and gas revenues as a means for resourcing otherwise underfunded public services, crafting a template of benchmarks for successful stabilization, and anticipating the need to apply constructive pressure to inhibit a flare-up of retributive violence against civilians.

None of these steps are panaceas, to be sure, and all are ultimately contingent upon how Eastern Syria's emerging mix of post-ISIS stakeholders view their interests in navigating toward a collaborative outcome—one that effectively precludes any resurgence of the Islamic State while also helping to set conditions for bringing Syria's long-running civil war to closure.

Acknowledgments

The authors of this report wish to thank U.S. policy practitioners in the Departments of State and Defense, and the U.S. Agency for International Development for sharing their insights regarding the highly complex, volatile issues currently in play in Eastern Syria. We also appreciate the expert perspectives offered by colleagues in the academic and public policy research communities, as well as by interlocutors from Syrian groups and international humanitarian organizations. Here at RAND, we are very grateful to our National Security Research Division and International Security and Defense Policy Center leadership for their strong support. Andrew Parasiliti and Michael McNerney offered helpful advice on the orchestration of this project's kick-off phase. We also benefited greatly from the peer reviews offered by Christopher Chivvis and Seth Jones on an earlier version of our analysis. And we greatly appreciate the vital assistance of Sarah Meadows, Barbara Hennessey, Katrina Griffin-Moore, Stacey Haughton, Pete Ledwich, and Matt Byrd in moving this report through RAND's administrative processes and Nora Spiering for her support in preparing this report for publication.

Abbreviations

CENTCOM	U.S. Central Command
cms	cubic meters per second
CVE	countering violent extremism
DoD	U.S. Department of Defense
FAO	Food and Agriculture Organization
ha	hectares
IDP	internally displaced person
IED	improvised explosive device
ISF	Iraqi Security Forces
ISIS	Islamic State of Iraq and Syria
MERV	Middle Euphrates River Valley
MODIS	moderate resolution imaging spectroradiometer
NDVI	Normalized Difference Vegetation Index
NGO	nongovernmental organization
NOAA	National Oceanic and Atmospheric Administration
PKK	Kurdistan Workers Party

SAC   Syrian Arab Coalition

SDF   Syrian Democratic Forces

UN   United Nations

UNOCHA   United Nations Office for the Coordination of
            Humanitarian Affairs

VEO   violent extremist organization

VIIRS   Visible Infrared Imaging Radiometer Suite

WFP   World Food Program

YPG   Yekîneyên Parastina Gel (People's Protection Units)

CHAPTER ONE

Introduction

The Islamic State's territorial hold on Eastern Syria has been virtually broken. Following Raqqah city's liberation in October 2017, the U.S.-supported Syrian Democratic Forces (SDF) pushed down from northern Kurdish areas along the northeast side of Syria's Euphrates River Valley, clearing Islamic State of Iraq and Syria (ISIS) fighters out of towns and villages and out of major oil and gas fields nearby. Meanwhile, Russian-backed pro-government forces pressed in from the West, first to free up their besieged military presence outside of the city of Deir ez-Zor and then to secure the region's three largest population centers, Deir ez-Zor city, Mayadin, and Abu Kamal. ISIS fighters had exercised de facto control over this region since 2014. The biggest question now looming for Euphrates Valley communities is how to navigate toward recovery given the enormous hardships and extremist violence they endured. As then–U.S. Central Command (CENTCOM) Commander Gen. Joseph Votel observed: "A lot of good military progress has been made . . . but the hard part I think is in front of us, and that is stabilizing these areas, consolidating gains, getting people back into their homes . . . ."[1]

On the civilian side, senior U.S. officials have also underscored locally focused stabilization in Syria's liberated areas as an essential element in the campaign to achieve a lasting defeat of ISIS.[2] While U.S.

---

[1] U.S. Institute of Peace, "Iraq and Syria: Views from the U.S. Administration, Military Leaders and the Region," panel discussion, Washington, D.C., April 3, 2018.

[2] Hoover Institution, "Secretary of State Rex W. Tillerson Discusses 'The Way Forward in Syria' with Condoleezza Rice," Stanford, Calif.: Stanford University, January 17, 2018.

President Donald Trump signaled his strong preference to withdraw U.S. forces from Syria and to get allies and partners to shoulder more of the recovery burdens, his stand against ISIS has been unwavering.[3] Internationally, he and Russian Federation President Vladimir Putin jointly indicated their strong support for the fight against ISIS while underscoring the value of deconfliction procedures to ensure the safety of U.S, Russian, and partner forces engaged in the fight against ISIS and to ultimately pursue a political solution to Syria's long-running civil war.[4]

Looking ahead, the ever-present challenge here is how best to translate U.S. policy preferences into an enduring approach to stability, given Syria's geopolitical volatility. With Moscow's backing, the Assad regime continues to press ahead on retaking rebel-held areas; Iran has expanded its proxies and influence in support of the Syrian government; and, in early 2018, Turkey launched a military campaign against Kurdish enclaves close to its border held by the Yekîneyên Parastina Gel (YPG [People's Protection Units]). The Turkish offensive lasted for several months and diverted Kurdish forces from their continued push against ISIS strongholds in Eastern Syria.[5] While the Kurdish-led SDF includes a significant number of Arab fighters, affiliated with the

---

The counter-ISIS coalition leadership has also reinforced this message (Operation Inherent Resolve, "Operation Inherent Resolve Update Brief with Maj. Gen. Gedney," December 27, 2017).

[3] Julie Hirschfeld Davis, "Trump Drops Push for Immediate Withdrawal of Troops from Syria," *New York Times*, April 4, 2018.

[4] Most notably, see U.S. Department of State, "Joint Statement by the President of the United States and the President of the Russian Federation," November 11, 2017. This joint statement also highlighted the value of "de-escalation areas"—i.e., venues where a cessation of hostilities and the movement of unarmed civilians could be implemented by both sides— but regime forces and their affiliates have largely disregarded that template, most recently in Syria's southwestern region.

[5] As then–Joint Staff Director Lt. Gen. McKenzie observed in a U.S. Department of Defense (DoD) press briefing, the Turkish campaign has "slowed down" the pace of SDF's advance in the Euphrates River Valley, though ISIS has not regained any momentum (U.S. Department of Defense, "Department of Defense Press Briefing by Pentagon Chief Spokesperson Dana W. White and Joint Staff Director Lt. Gen. Kenneth F. McKenzie Jr. in the Pentagon Briefing Room," March 15, 2018a).

Syrian Arab Coalition (SAC), the Turkish government considers the YPG to be linked to the Kurdistan Workers Party (PKK). Ankara and Washington both consider the PKK to be a terrorist group.

In furtherance of U.S. policy goals, and building on RAND's prior analyses,[6] this report assesses post-ISIS stabilization challenges along Syria's Middle Euphrates River Valley (MERV),[7] which stretches southeast from Raqqah for over 250 kilometers through Deir ez-Zor city (the broader governorate shares the same name) down to the Syria-Iraq border.[8] See Figure 1.1 for a snapshot of the MERV's geography and demography. Two overarching questions are addressed:

1. What are the most urgent local needs that stabilization efforts should address?
2. Is there a viable strategy for orchestrating near-term stabilization in a region where forces aligned in different coalitions are holding opposite sides of the Euphrates Valley?

This report aims to help planners and policy practitioners prioritize critical needs for locally focused stabilization efforts in the MERV. It also identifies key challenges that stabilization efforts must overcome in a region where the key actors share an interest in defeating ISIS but find themselves on opposing sides of other contentious issues, including the character of the regime in Damascus, control over resources, and the degree of local autonomy.

---

[6] Illustratively, see Shelly Culbertson and Linda Robinson, *Making Victory Count After Defeating ISIS: Stabilization Challenges in Mosul and Beyond*, Santa Monica, Calif.: RAND Corporation, RR-2076-RC, 2017; Eric Robinson, Daniel Egel, Patrick B. Johnston, Sean Mann, Alexander D. Rothenberg, and David Stebbins, *When the Islamic State Comes to Town: The Economic Impact of Islamic State Governance in Iraq and Syria*, Santa Monica, Calif.: RAND Corporation, RR-1970-RC, 2017; and a number of other reports.

[7] The MERV is not a term used by Syrians to describe this geography. Syrians commonly talk about al-Jazirah (the Peninsula), by which they are referencing the expanse of territory east of the Euphrates river up to the Tigris. The less populated territory outside of the river valley to the west of the Euphrates is referred to as al-Badiya.

[8] Defined more regionally, the MERV stretches farther, down to the city of Haditha in Anbar province, Iraq. This report covers only the MERV's Syrian portion.

Figure 1.1
Syria's Middle Euphrates River Valley in Deir ez-Zor Governorate

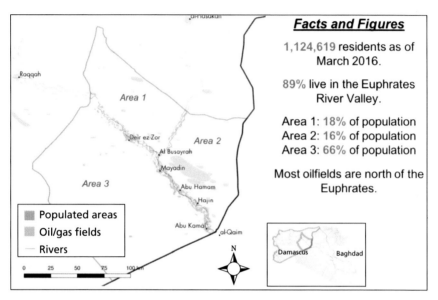

SOURCE: Data from Oak Ridge National Laboratory LandScan, 2016.

The Context of a Stabilization Mission in the MERV

In developing a policy for supporting locally focused stabilization in Eastern Syria, three challenges should be flagged up front. First, there is the unavoidable issue of expectations. After living under the Islamic State's control for over three years, liberated communities in the MERV are likely asking: Are we better off now than we were under ISIS? Given the Islamic State's disastrous management of the governorate—which included the killing of opponents, mismanagement of water, and shortages of electricity—it is hard to imagine anything other than a pervasive sense of relief throughout the Valley. Nevertheless, as local populations strive to fend off the reemergence of jihadi extremism, communities need a tangible sense that they are navigating toward a quality of life that exceeds their levels of security, governance, and economic well-being prior to 2014, when ISIS consolidated its control there. As a historically peripheral, underserved region in Syria, the MERV's pre-2014 legacies cannot be ignored in the fight to sustainably defeat ISIS, no matter who ends up controlling Eastern Syria's vast expanse.

Anticipating such comparisons is vitally important for prioritizing on-the-ground programs and shaping overall benchmarks for performance. U.S. officials have characterized post-ISIS stabilization in Syria and Iraq as narrowly scoped endeavors—basically, to secure liberated areas, to provide humanitarian relief to local communities, and to restore basic public services—and not as investments in reconstruction or nation-building.[9] These near-term priorities are critical steps, to be sure. The harder question is how they can give traction to locally led, longer-term efforts aimed at achieving levels of security, governance, public services, and economic viability that would effectively preclude opportunities for ISIS's reemergence. For Syria, the only feasible pathway toward that end requires a closure to its larger, long-running civil war.

A second challenge that post-ISIS recovery efforts need to address is the imperative of countering violent extremism. While stabilization has never conformed to a "one size fits all" template, the norm in most conflict-affected venues has been to facilitate engagements between hitherto hostile but ultimately reconcilable actors. Yet, given their extremist ideology, it is hard to imagine that the ISIS cohort would ever self-identify as reconcilable with any group they view as apostate. And while their hold on territory has slipped away, residual ISIS fighters are still present and are resorting to guerilla tactics. That raises concerns regarding community vulnerability to radicalizing influences—especially among young males—as well as suspicions regarding a lingering presence of ISIS sympathizers, all of which increase the potential for retributive violence as anti-ISIS forces move in. And that risk is shared on both sides of the river as either regime or SDF-aligned forces could use this threat as a pretext for heavy-handed tactics, and those families that suffered at the hands of ISIS may seek revenge against others they perceive as having aided and abetted ISIS control.

Thirdly, and more broadly, planners should anticipate that stabilization-centric transitions often generate their own instabilities.

---

[9] Hoover Institution, 2018.

Of greatest relevance for Eastern Syria: The security forces that have cleared ISIS fighters from the MERV will need to hand off responsibilities to a "hold" force that provides internal security until local police capacity can be regenerated. How will that force be viewed locally? Also, governance duties will become the writ of local civilian councils, typically composed of tribal elders or other community representatives. Will these bodies be seen as legitimate? In addition, refugees and IDPs will likely be flooding back into their communities. Will these returnees catalyze disputes over land tenure, anxieties about ISIS reinfiltration, or community flare-ups fueled by "Why did they leave while I stayed?" narratives. And, finally, progress on restoring transit routes could help revive local markets but could also open pathways for illicit trafficking, smuggling, and criminal activity more generally.

While none of these phenomena are fundamentally new in the stabilization arena, each will exert a degree of influence on Eastern Syria's post-ISIS landscape and thus should be factored into stabilization planning as the process moves forward.

Methods, Sources, and Scope of This Report

This report addresses Eastern Syria's stabilization challenges via a three-step progression. Drawing on extensive research conducted in 2017 and 2018, our analysis opens with a sociocultural profile of the MERV's demography. Second, this report assesses enduring needs in the MERV's populated areas, based on a multisectoral analysis of key dimensions of community well-being that are featured in stabilization's foundational documents and which, if prioritized, may help to galvanize progress toward the MERV'S early recovery.[10] The data drawn upon for this analysis include unclassified satellite imagery and remote

---

[10]   This report examines conflict-related impacts across seven sectors. Four of these include infrastructure and natural resources (building damage, electricity availability, petrochemical production, and water resources); a fifth focuses on geopolitical impacts (human displacement); and the last two sectors focus on economic activity (market activity and agricultural production). All fall within stabilization's traditional template. See, for example, U.S. Institute of Peace and the U.S. Army War College, Peacekeeping and Stability Operations Insti-

sensing data, as well as publicly available reports from U.S. and international agencies and nongovernmental organizations (NGOs).

Regarding data sources, remotely sensed information offers the benefit of being a primary source for this analysis, rather than a secondary one, as well as a neutral information source. Satellite imagery, nighttime lighting, and estimates of agricultural production derived from remote sensing are complemented and corroborated, whenever possible, by open-source news articles, published academic work, and reports from international aid and response organizations. That said, remote sensing is also subject to constraints. Visual inspection may be limited by the temporal availability of satellite images, the clarity of those images (e.g., the presence of clouds), and the analyst's interpretation of the images. We attempted to limit errors by validating observed damages with reporting and documentation of activities in the vicinity. In the agricultural sector, the vegetative index–based estimates are widely used in the planning and engineering contexts, as well as in measuring production, but this approach is also limited by the clarity and spatial resolution of the raw images. Finally, nighttime lighting is a metric often used to estimate electricity provision and usage. Errors in nighttime lighting estimates could stem from the timing at which satellites pass over the region. However, consistency in satellite orbital patterns often leads to a somewhat consistent pass time, allowing us to compare changes from time period to time period.

As these multiple data sources help to provide a solid evidentiary base for assessing the impact of damages that MERV communities have endured, this report moves into the geopolitical sphere for the third step. It analyzes the key operational choices that stakeholders would need to consider if they opt to orchestrate post-ISIS stabilization efforts in a region where regime and nonregime forces are both present. The sources here include unclassified reporting provided by U.S. government stakeholders and preliminary assessments of efforts by external parties and their local partners to orchestrate agreed deconfliction and de-escalation zones elsewhere in Syria.

---

tute, *Guiding Principles for Stabilization and Reconstruction*, Washington, D.C.: USIP Press, 2009.

Drawing conclusions from these domains, the report wraps up by highlighting a sequence of recommended actions for advancing MERV-centric stabilization. While our research was conducted during the 2017–2018 time frame, as noted above, Eastern Syria's stabilization challenges nevertheless exhibit certain enduring qualities even in a highly volatile political context. Although we do not delve into the broader challenges of achieving a lasting peace settlement to Syria's larger civil war—e.g., criminal justice proceedings, the costs of nationwide reconstruction, or the repatriation of foreign ISIS fighters and their families to their countries of origin—progress on charting a pathway toward the MERV's recovery would surely be a positive step toward longer-term peace and stability.

CHAPTER TWO

The MERV in Perspective

The design and execution of any successful stabilization effort in Deir ez-Zor will need to account for the governorate's sociocultural context, by which the authors of this report mean the ways in which the people of Deir ez-Zor self-identify, relate to one another, and mobilize. While this report is focused on contemporary Deir ez-Zor, its sociocultural context has been deeply influenced by the authorities (i.e., the Ottomans, the French Mandate, earlier Syrian governments) that have administered this governorate in the past,[1] as well as the informal authority exercised by different actors during the country's last decade of civil conflict. The picture of Deir ez-Zor that emerges from these experiences is exceedingly complex. Amidst its intricate mosaic of tribal communities, the governorate's formal state-run institutions exercised more administrative authority than its tribal elders in the decades prior to the rise of ISIS in 2014. This reality suggests that any outside power seeking to exert influence in Deir ez-Zor will struggle to outmaneuver the Syrian government while also contending with a highly fractured governorate featuring rivalries and conflicts that predate the 2011 uprising and are likely to persist after the conclusion of the civil war.

---

[1]   For a foundational treatment of Syria's sociocultural context, see Hanna Batatu, *Syria's Peasantry, the Descendants of Its Less Rural Notables, and Their Politics*, Princeton, N.J.: Princeton University Press, 1999.

Impact of Historic Efforts to Administer Deir ez-Zor

While this report cannot provide a comprehensive treatment of Deir ez-Zor's history, it can help U.S. policymakers and planners understand the impact of central administration on the governorate's evolution. Whether one takes the late Ottoman Empire, the French Mandate period, or the Syrian state as the point of reference, a common theme is each power's attempt to break or channel tribal authority to reinforce central control over the governorate.[2] By all accounts, Deir ez-Zor is a highly tribal governorate. But the character of tribalism in Deir ez-Zor has been impacted by two centuries of effort to co-opt, settle, and divide tribes. The strategies employed depend on the particular central authority, but they encompass the establishment of property rights to provide a basis for taxation, the granting of property and exemption of military service to preferred tribal leaders to sow division and create an incentive for tribal sheikhs to solicit the favor of the central authority, the forced settlement of tribes, and the prevention of the relocation of tribes to western areas of Syria from which they would pose a more immediate threat to the state's central administration.[3] Not all policies were equally coercive; indeed, the Assad regime has often granted a degree of local autonomy to tribal leaders in return for allegiance to the state.

In addition to various policies used to co-opt the tribes, each authority also promoted ideologies that were designed to cultivate a political culture that would move Syria beyond tribalism. So whether the impetus was the *tanzimat* (Ottoman reforms) adopted to modernize state administration when that empire was feeling pressured by European advances in the 19th century, or the creation of the modern Syrian state under the French Mandate, or the pan-Arabism embodied in the shorter-lived United Arab Republic, or the evolution of Baath

---

[2] Dawn Chatty, "Al-Qaba'il wa al-Qabaliya wa al-Hawiya al-Siyasiya fi Suriya al-Mu'asira" ("The Tribes, Tribalism, and Political Identity in Contemporary Syria"), *Omran Journal for Sociology and Anthropology*, Vol. 4, No. 15, January 2016, pp. 81–96.

[3] See Kheder Khaddour and Kevin Mazur, "Eastern Expectations: The Changing Dynamics in Syria's Tribal Regions," Carnegie Endowment for International Peace, February 28, 2017.

Party rule in Syria, for which its identity politics privileged ethnicity (Arabism) over tribe or sect, all of these authorities were promoting alternatives to tribal structures.

The priority given to limiting tribal authority validates the premise that tribalism was a significant force in the governorate that central authorities felt compelled to address. But two centuries of efforts to harness this force have had an impact on what tribalism means in present-day Eastern Syria. The impacts are several. First, tribal sheikhs no longer exercise strong authority over tribal members. This is particularly true at the most aggregated level—the confederation—but also at the tribe, subtribe, and clan levels. Simply put, tribal sheikhs cannot "deliver" their members. For example, the strongest tribal confederation in the governorate is the ʿEgaidat, and people who self-identify as part of the confederation span pro-regime, pro-opposition, pro-ISIS, and every other meaningful affiliation. No paramount sheikh can move the ʿEgaidat, and so while it will behoove U.S. policymakers and planners to be aware of the confederation and its weight, it is not a meaningful unit of analysis in the sense that members cannot be reduced to a specific political disposition, nor do the ʿEgaidat operate collectively.[4]

Second, the power of tribal sheikhs has been diluted to the extent that sheikhs who show opposition to competing sources of authority are often forced to capitulate to those forces, lest their members join with those competing authorities, further undermining their ability to claim to represent any constituency.[5] The state, foreign powers, and armed groups have undermined tribal authorities by strong-arming sheikhs who oppose their projects. So, if the United States seeks to work through tribal leaders to stabilize portions of the governorate held

---

[4]   An illustrative example are the different experiences of the Bakir, Mashhada, and Shaytat, all tribes within the ʿEgaidat confederation, with ISIS. In general, it is believed that Bakir tribal militias more commonly aligned with ISIS than Mashhada or Shaytat militias did, but even at the tribal level, there were split alignments (Nicholas Heras, Bassam Barabandi, and Nidal Betare, *Deir Azzour Tribal Mapping Project*, Washington, D.C.: Center for a New American Security, September 2017).

[5]   For a good description of how ISIS demoralized those in Deir ez-Zor who resisted their rule, see Heras, Barabandi, and Betare, 2017, p. 5.

by U.S. partners (i.e., the SDF), it is important to understand that these same tribal leaders have often "lost" in their confrontations with competing sources of power, including relatively weak violent extremist organizations (VEOs) like Jabhat an-Nusra. This should give U.S. policymakers and planners pause in presuming that tribal leaders will be able to secure the peace.

The Civil War's Impact on Deir ez-Zor's Sociocultural Context

The process by which tribal authority has been constrained and fractured was accelerated by the civil war in Syria that led to parts of Deir ez-Zor falling to a mix of opposition groups and terrorist factions, and eventually falling to ISIS in 2014. This is counterintuitive to those who assume that a vacuum of authority and insecurity increases tribalism as locals revert to these identities. In Deir ez-Zor, however, the retreat of the regime did not increase the authority of sheikhly families as the *de facto* authorities and providers of security. On the contrary, opposition forces, ISIS, and regime loyalists recruited upstarts to promote their aims in the governorate (e.g., territorial control, freedom of movement, access to oil revenues), and when traditional tribal authorities opposed these actions, they worked to divide tribes by recruiting clans and subtribes within them or by humiliating traditional tribal leaders by forcing them to submit, flee, pay tributes, or have their tribes be subjected to violent reprisals, including mass executions.[6]

This context creates at least as much risk as opportunity should the United States seek to operate through tribes to secure support for local administrative councils north and east of the Euphrates or to man security forces to stabilize "liberated areas." The risks are manifold. First, tribes cannot be meaningfully binned as "pro-coalition" "pro regime," or "ISIS sympathizers." There are extreme examples like

6   Al-Hayat, "Najun Yarawun lil Marra al-Uwla Waqa'a' Qatl 800 fi Majzarat 'Ashirat al-Shaytat" ("The Saved See for the First Time the Evidence of the Killing of 800 in the Massacre of the Shaytat Tribe"), October 3, 2014.

the Shaytat, a tribe that suffered horrific attacks by ISIS and thus are strongly opposed to the group. But most tribes had individual members in all camps and will not move in unison. A second challenge is that other relevant actors have deeper knowledge of the area's sociocultural context and a longer history than the United States of trying to work through it. The regime and Iran have even gone as far as to promote conversion to Shi'ism, with a degree of success,[7] as a way to project influence in an otherwise strongly Sunni-Arab region. And, as was noted in Figure 1.1, it is the regime, with Russian and Iranian support, that now controls roughly two-thirds of the governorate's population (Area 3), which will provide them an additional advantage in building local ties—tribal or otherwise—to advance their aims.

Another challenge, as noted earlier, is that the Syrian government has formal institutions in place in Deir ez-Zor that have had previous experience in administering the governorate, albeit coercively. For example, the former governor of Deir ez-Zor, Mohamad Ibrahim Samra, more commonly known by locals as Abu Muhannad, was a general in Assad's Interior Ministry before being appointed to the governor's post in 2016. Samra also had experience in administering the governorate of Deir ez-Zor, having previously directed a subdistrict called At-Tabani, which is north of Deir ez-Zor city on the Raqqah governorate border.[8] Given his security background, Samra was believed to have strong ties to formal and informal security actors aligned with the regime that have taken the western side of the Euphrates in Deir ez-Zor. And as the official representative of the Assad regime in the governorate, Samra spoke with authority about the regime's recon-

---

[7]   Iran is reported to have converted the Baqir Brigade from Bari al-Halbiya tribe members. Iran has also mobilized a militia from Shi'a Baggara (a tribal confederation) influenced by Sheikh Nawaf al-Bashir, a former regime oppositionist who has switched allegiances in the conflict. See Asharq al-Awsat, "Kharitat al Milishiat al-Iraniya fi Suriya" ("The Map of Iranian Militias in Syria"), August 23, 2017. For a corroborating account of the role of Nawaf al-Bashir, see Heras, Barabandi, and Betare, 2017, p. 4. For an estimate of the proportion of the Baggara converted to Shi'ism via Iranian financed efforts, see Chatty (2016), which puts the figure at 25 percent.

[8]   Micro Syria, "Nahwa Mazid min al-'Askara: Al-Liwa'Abu Muhannad Samra Muhafizhan lama Tabqa min Deir Ezzour" ("Towards Additional Militarization: General Abu Muhannad Is the Governor of What Remains of Deir Ezzour"), October 27, 2016.

struction plans. For instance, in late 2017, he noted that the regime had set aside the equivalent of US$12 million to rehabilitate the water and electricity networks in Deir ez-Zor city.[9]

As the United States seeks to complete its counter-ISIS mission, it lacks the equivalent administration to work through—having to rely on still-nascent local civilian councils—to partner in any future stabilization mission. And while the Assad regime has a serious legitimacy gap among parts of the governorate's population, so do U.S. partners, with the SDF or its local incarnation, the Deir ez-Zor Military Council, often derided by Sunni Arabs as a front for Kurdish territorial ambitions.[10]

Given these complexities, locally focused stabilization efforts throughout the governorate are going to be challenging. On the planning side, the task of assessing who enjoys legitimacy will inevitably be a community-by-community undertaking. Any presumption that sheikhs will be able to exercise authority to govern or effectively mediate disputes across larger populated areas within their tribal ambit may not prove viable. Ultimately, those actors who exercise the greatest sway in facilitating community-level efforts toward economic recovery and the restoration of public services may prove to be the most influential. For external partners, the key here will be to ensure that stabilization investments are inclusive, transparent, and not seen as favoring one group at the expense of another. Otherwise, such efforts would risk sowing greater divisions among communities to the benefit of would-be spoilers.

---

[9]   RT Arabic News, "Muhafizh Deir Ez Zour Yuhadid Takalif I'adat Bina' al-Madina" ("The Governor of Deir Ezzour Determines the Cost of the City's Reconstruction"), November 8, 2017.

[10]   For a particularly strong attack on the SDF, see Orient Research Centre, "Sharqi Suriya bayn Qasd wa al-Assad" ("Eastern Syria Between the SDF and Assad"), undated. For a more measured critique, see Nicholas Heras and Omar Abu Layla, "The Security Vacuum in Post-ISIS Deir Ezzor," *Syria Deeply*, November 15, 2017.

CHAPTER THREE

Assessing the Region's Critical Needs

This chapter provides a stabilization needs assessment for the Deir ez-Zor governorate, surveying multidomain evidence regarding the status of its critical infrastructure, natural resources, local populations, and economic activity across the region.

We focus on seven key sectors of Deir ez-Zor's public services and local economy, grouped into three main categories, as summarized in Table 3.1. We examine stabilization needs in each sector using a combination of satellite imagery, remote sensing data, and secondary data sources, such as U.S., UN, and NGO reporting. Within each of these sectors, we examine three broad themes:

1. **How well did ISIS manage this sector earlier in the conflict?** A clear understanding of conditions in the MERV under ISIS is necessary to gauge local expectations for a post-ISIS recovery.

2. **What level of wartime damage has this sector endured?** Even if local economies functioned properly under ISIS control, the campaign to liberate the MERV has proven costly to physical infrastructure. Damage to such infrastructure could complicate long-term recovery and, at a minimum, should dictate priorities for short-term assistance.

3. **Compared with other liberated cities in Syria, what are the right performance benchmarks for stabilization?** Recovery from conflict should be measured in months, if not years. The experience of previously liberated cities elsewhere in Syria can set realistic expectations for the pace of recovery in the MERV going forward.

Table 3.1
Measuring Deir ez-Zor's Stabilization Needs

Category	Sector	Description	Data Source
Infrastructure and natural resources	Infrastructure damage	Level of damage of hospitals, bridges, markets, industrial facilities, transit facilities, and electricity substations	Satellite imagery, 10/2017–11/2017
	Electricity	Levels of electricity consumption, measured using nighttime lighting from NOAA's VIIRS satellite data	Remote sensing data, 1/2014–9/2017
	Oil and gas resources	Geographic laydown of oil resources and pipelines	Open-source data and U.S. government reporting, 2/2016–12/2017
	Water resources	Status of water treatment facilities based on satellite imagery	Satellite imagery, 11/2015–6/2017
Population	IDP flows	Population levels by city, displacement trends by governorate, and imagery analysis of growth in IDP camps	Remote sensing data, UNOCHA and NGO data, and satellite imagery, 7/2017–5/2018
Economic activity	Market activity	Activity levels at main market areas	Satellite imagery 5/2017–11/2017
	Agricultural production	Historical and current agricultural productivity, measured using NDVI	Remote sensing data, 1/2009–9/2017

NOTES: NDVI = Normalized Difference Vegetation Index. NOAA = National Oceanic and Atmospheric Administration. UNOCHA = UN Office for the Coordination of Humanitarian Affairs. VIIRS = Visible Infrared Imaging Radiometer Suite.

In assessing stabilization needs, there is an all-pervasive threat that remote imagery cannot capture: a lethal mix of booby traps, landmines, and improvised explosive devices (IEDs) that fleeing ISIS fighters have likely planted in and around critical infrastructure, schools, hospitals, markets, and local neighborhoods. As seen in Raqqah, Syria; Mosul, Iraq; and other venues, ISIS fighters have sought to ensure that their flight would not end their fight against apostate enemies. These explosive hazards have inflicted casualties on security forces in their operations to clear ISIS fighters block by block, house by house, or even room by room. And, tragically, these hazards also pose a major barrier to the safe return of displaced civilians to their home communities. Consequently, the time and likely costs associated with the clearance of unexploded ordnance need to be factored into stabilization and recovery efforts, both in public venues and private residential areas.[1]

Infrastructure and Natural Resources

We first examine the status of the Deir ez-Zor governorate's critical infrastructure and natural resources.

Status of Critical Infrastructure

RAND researchers used satellite imagery to assess the level of damage to 51 pieces of critical infrastructure in the Deir ez-Zor governorate's three largest cities—Abu Kamal, Mayadin, and Deir ez-Zor city. These points of interest included two major electricity substations, 13 bridges, 12 hospitals, 16 markets, five major industrial facilities, and three transit facilities.[2] Figure 3.1 shows the level of damage to this infrastructure based on November 2017 satellite imagery. As of that time frame, the vast majority of bridges, markets, and industrial facilities in these cities had been damaged or destroyed. Perhaps surprisingly, only two of the 12 hospitals in the governorate showed clear signs of damage.

In the more rural regions of Deir Ez-Zor governorate, particularly on the eastern side of the Euphrates River, a significant number of large facilities and a large portion of the region's critical infrastructure showed signs of damage in satellite imagery of early 2018. In the

---

[1] Field reports from July 2018 indicated that the scale and geographical scope of explosive hazards remained dangerously high in Deir ez-Zor governorate (UNOCHA, "Syria Crisis: Northeast Syria Situation Report No. 26 [15 June–15 July 2018]," July 2018c).

[2] The authors relied on existing open-source mapping data from Wikimapia, supplemented by prior RAND research and a manual analysis of satellite imagery of each city. While the resulting roster of key infrastructure is likely not exhaustive, especially in the electricity sector, where substations are not always readily visible via overhead imagery, we believe it is broadly representative (Wikimapia, undated; Robinson et al., 2017).

Figure 3.1
Critical Infrastructure Damage in Deir ez-Zor, Mayadin, and Abu Kamal,
November 2017

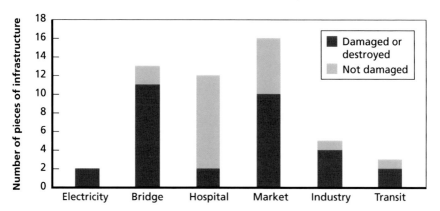

SOURCES: Data from imagery from DigitalGlobe, 2017. Locations identified using Wikimapia, undated, and Robinson et al., 2017.
NOTE: Estimates are based on manual analysis of satellite imagery captured in October and November 2017.

large industrial zone along National Highway N-7, nearly all facilities, including the sugar factory in Figure 3.2, appeared inoperable and no longer in use because of substantial physical damage. Further south near Abu Hamam, destruction at a storage facility near the Kahara Air Base in Figure 3.3 appears to have occurred in September 2017, while operation ceased around June 2017.

In Deir ez-Zor city, the vast majority of damage to key infrastructure exists in former ISIS-held neighborhoods in the eastern half of the city.[3] Eight of the city's ten bridges were damaged or destroyed, including both bridges crossing the Euphrates River. In Abu Kamal, the city's largest grain storage facility showed heavy signs of damage in imagery from early November 2017. And in Mayadin, similar damage to critical infrastructure can be seen in Figure 3.4.

Despite major damage to the governorate's bridges, the level of damage seen in Deir ez-Zor, Mayadin, and Abu Kamal is actually

---

[3]   This comports with older estimates of damage in Deir ez-Zor city from mid-2016 in Robinson et al., 2017.

Figure 3.2
Damage to Sugar Factory in Industrial Zone on N-7 National Highway, Eastern Side of Euphrates Near Deir ez-Zor City

July 2012   December 2017

SOURCES: Wikimapia, undated; DigitalGlobe, accessed January 3, 2018.

Figure 3.3
Damage to Storage Facility Near Kahara Air Base in Abu Hamam

May 2017   December 2017

SOURCES: Wikimapia, undated; DigitalGlobe, accessed January 5, 2018.

modest compared with the extensive physical damage seen in Raqqah at the end of the bloody campaign to liberate the city. Every single one of the city's main bridges, market facilities, and major industrial facilities was damaged or destroyed, as seen in satellite imagery from November 2017. Where hospitals went largely unscathed in Mayadin,

Figure 3.4
Damage to Infrastructure in Mayadin, November 2017

Mayadin Gas Company   Euphrates Bridge

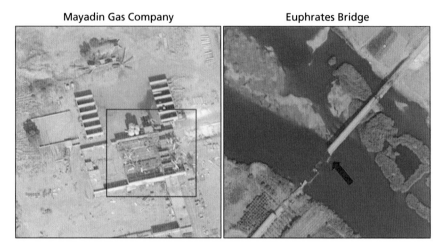

SOURCES: Wikimapia, undated; DigitalGlobe, November 7, 2017.

Abu Kamal, and Deir ez-Zor, two-thirds of Raqqah's hospitals were destroyed during the extended fight to clear the city.

Instead, the level of damage seen in the Deir ez-Zor region is much more comparable to that seen in neighboring Tabqa. That city experienced major damage to its northern industrial areas under ISIS control (dating back to at least mid-2016), but only minor damage to its main market area and main hospital.[4]

Electricity Consumption
We measure electricity consumption using nighttime lighting data, made available by NOAA on a monthly basis since January 2014.[5]

---

[4] DigitalGlobe, imagery from July 6, 2016, and October 24, 2017.

[5] For more information on the use of nighttime lighting as a measure of electricity consumption, see Robinson et al., 2017; and Daniel Egel, Charles P. Ries, Ben Connable, Todd Helmus, Eric Robinson, Isaac Baruffi, Melissa A. Bradley, Kurt Card, Kathleen Loa, Sean Mann, Fernando Sedano, Stephan B. Seabrook, and Robert Stewart, *Investing in the Fight: Assessing the Use of the Commander's Emergency Response Program in Afghanistan*, Santa Monica, Calif.: RAND Corporation, RR-1508-OSD, 2016.

These data capture the intensity of light at night as a proxy for electricity supply and demand.

Figure 3.5 shows this analysis of nighttime lighting over Deir ez-Zor governorate and surrounding areas in January 2014 and September 2017. Although most of the governorate is dark at night (shown in black), the stretch of the MERV from Deir ez-Zor city to the Syria-Iraq border showed signs of significant nighttime lighting in pre-ISIS January 2014. However, by September 2017, nighttime lighting had fallen by 95 percent in Deir ez-Zor city, by 82 percent in Mayadin, and by 92 percent in Abu Kamal. Similar reductions occurred in Raqqah (97 percent) and Aleppo (81 percent) over this same period.

Electricity availability in Deir ez-Zor under ISIS control was paltry at best, despite the group's dominance over the region's oil resources. Figure 3.6 shows nighttime lighting levels in Deir ez-Zor, Mayadin, and Abu Kamal for each month since January 2014. ISIS gained a foothold in all three cities at roughly the same time period in June 2014, and the major declines in electricity consumption were soon to follow.

Deir ez-Zor city has fared the worst since then, operating in the dark since April 2015. Mayadin and Abu Kamal have fared slightly better, with nighttime lighting in October 2016 at or near 90 percent and 50 percent of pre-ISIS levels, respectively. The resulting precipitous

Figure 3.5
Nighttime Lighting in Deir ez-Zor Governorate, January 2014 and September 2017

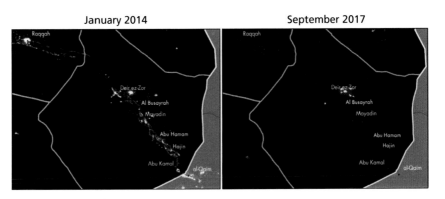

January 2014   September 2017

SOURCE: Data from NOAA, VIIRS, 2014–2017.

Figure 3.6
Nighttime Lighting in Deir ez-Zor, Mayadin, and Abu Kamal

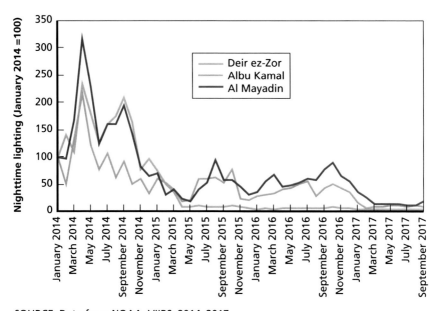

SOURCE: Data from NOAA, VIIRS, 2014–2017.

decline in electricity consumption in all three cities over the course of 2017 suggests that military pressure on the governorate in recent months has been a critical factor driving declines in electricity consumption.

We can also use nighttime lighting to measure how quickly electricity can be reconstituted in a newly liberated city. Figure 3.7 shows the pace of electricity recovery in the first few months after liberation for Manbij (liberated in August 2016), al-Bab (liberated in March 2017), and Tabqa (liberated in May 2017). Nighttime lighting estimates are normalized to their pre-ISIS levels as of January 2014, such that an increase of 100 points along the y axis represents a 100-percent gain in nighttime lighting relative to January 2014 levels.

Figure 3.7 paints a strikingly more negative picture for Tabqa than for the other two cities in this figure, showing glacial progress at returning the city to pre-ISIS levels of electricity consumption. Al-Bab, which was liberated by Turkey and Syrian opposition groups

Figure 3.7
Pace of Electricity Recovery Post-Liberation

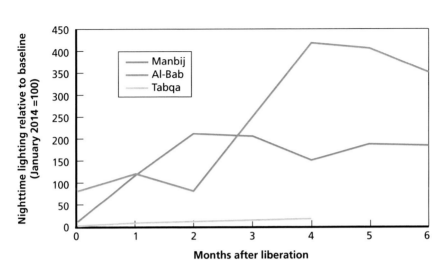

SOURCE: Data from NOAA, VIIRS, 2014–2017.
NOTES: Manbij and Jarabulus were liberated in August 2016. Al-Bab was liberated in March 2017. Tabqa was liberated in May 2017. Manbij and Tabqa were liberated by the SDF, while Jarabulus and al-Bab were liberated by Turkish-backed Syrian Opposition forces.

in March 2017, had flat nighttime lighting for the first two months after the city was liberated before a period of rapid growth soon thereafter. However, the city's electricity consumption was already at or near pre-ISIS levels upon its liberation, suggesting that reconstituting the city's power supply was less of a challenge than elsewhere.[6] In contrast, Manbij was pitch black upon its liberation by the SDF in August 2016, but it showed a similarly rapid recovery in electricity consumption soon thereafter.

This analysis suggests that the pace of rebuilding the electrical grid is not likely to be identical across cities.

---

[6] Furthermore, at least in the case of Jarabulus, Turkey successfully ran power lines across its southern border and into Northern Syria. Six months after the city's liberation, nighttime lighting had risen 327 percent above its levels at liberation, the highest seen in that region. See Suraj Sharma, "Turkey Sends Power Lines into Syrian Town Cleared of IS," *Middle East Eye*, September 8, 2016.

Oil and Gas Resources

Although the vast majority of Deir ez-Zor's population lives along the fertile banks of the Euphrates River, the economic focal point of the governorate lies in its vast oil and natural gas reserves. Deir ez-Zor was once responsible for an estimated 70 percent of the $4.1 billion in annual revenues from oil and gas production in Syria.[7] At its peak, the Islamic State generated $250 million to $365 million annually from oil fields across its caliphate, the majority of which was concentrated in Deir ez-Zor.[8] An investigation by the *Financial Times* in 2015 revealed that ISIS was extracting 34,000 to 40,000 barrels per day of oil in the governorate, according to local estimates.[9]

Figure 3.8 shows the location of known oil and gas fields across Deir ez-Zor. The largest fields, both in geographic scope and size of physical reserves, lie to the northeast of the Euphrates River and east of the Khabur River. The largest two fields, at Tanak and Omar, were responsible for roughly half of Deir ez-Zor's total oil production in 2015, according to the *Financial Times*. Based on local sale prices at the time of $40 to $45 per barrel, this would amount to over $800,000 a day in revenue-generating potential (or nearly $300 million annually).[10] To the extent that the SDF has cleared and holds this territory, these oil resources offer significant leverage in future negotiations with the regime. At a minimum, they offer a major source of short-term revenue to whomever controls the spigot.

Even though most fields lie northeast of the Euphrates, the primary demand for these resources once extracted comes from the popu-

---

[7] Phil Sands, "Oil, Food and Protest in Syria's Restive East," *The National*, January 17, 2012.

[8] Yeganeh Torbati, "Islamic State Yearly Oil Revenue Halved to $250 million: U.S. Official," *Reuters*, May 11, 2016; Benoit Faucon and Margaret Coker, "The Rise and Deadly Fall of Islamic State's Oil Tycoon," *Wall Street Journal*, April 24, 2016.

[9] Erika Solomon, Robin Kwong, and Steven Bernard, "Inside ISIS Inc: The Journey of a Barrel of Oil," *Financial Times*, February 29, 2016.

[10] Solomon, Kwong, and Bernard, 2016. Absent the sustained air campaign inhibiting ISIS's oil production (known as Operation Tidal Wave II), and with unfettered access to the global oil market at higher prices, it would be reasonable to expect higher revenues from oil production in Deir ez-Zor going forward.

Figure 3.8
Major Oil and Gas Resources in Deir ez-Zor Governorate

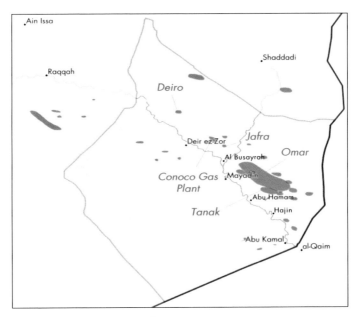

SOURCE: Wikimapia, undated.

lous and regime-held western areas of Syria. Figure 3.9 shows a map of the major oil and natural gas pipelines in Syria, the origins of which are heavily concentrated in the MERV and traverse westward toward Homs, Damascus, and Latakia.

Investigative reporting by the *Financial Times* revealed that ISIS and the Syrian government reached a quid pro quo agreement for the group to continue selling oil and gas resources to the regime in exchange for cash payments, technical expertise, and sustained market access.[11] Without these energy resources to power parts of Syria under its control, the Assad regime's grip over restive Sunni areas in the western half of the country may have proven less steady. In the future, it would be reasonable to expect the regime to pursue a similar arrangement with

---

[11] Erika Solomon and Ahmed Mhidi, "ISIS Inc: Syria's 'Mafia-Style' Gas Deals with Jihadis," *Financial Times*, October 15, 2015.

Figure 3.9
Pipeline Infrastructure in Syria

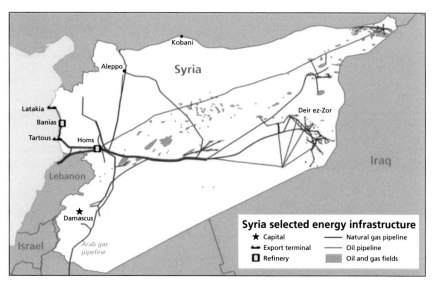

SOURCE: U.S. Energy Information Administration, undated.

whomever operates Deir ez-Zor's oil and gas fields, whether Kurdish, Sunni Arab, or regime-backed militias.

In the Omar and Marad oil fields, on the eastern side of the Euphrates River, a significant proportion of oil and gas facilities have been either damaged or completely destroyed, according to visual inspection of satellite imagery. Furthermore, nearly all facilities appeared to be underoperating or nonoperational. Figure 3.10 shows a destroyed thermal natural gas power plant in the western Omar oil field that was likely a source of power for a significant portion of the surrounding industrial and oil and gas facilities. Farther south and to the east of Abu Hamam, Figure 3.11 illustrates further damage to oil facilities in the region. The crude oil production facility shown in this figure indicates leakage and underperformance in May 2016 (left), and in December 2017 (right) it shows damage to both of the retention ponds for crude oil (upper right of the image), as well as destruction of much of the remaining production infrastructure.

Figure 3.10
Damage to Thermal Natural Gas Power Plant, Omar Oil Field

April 2016   November 2017

SOURCE: Wikimapia, undated; DigitalGlobe, accessed January 3, 2018.

Figure 3.11
Damage to Crude Oil Production Facilities in Marad Oil Field

May 2016   December 2017

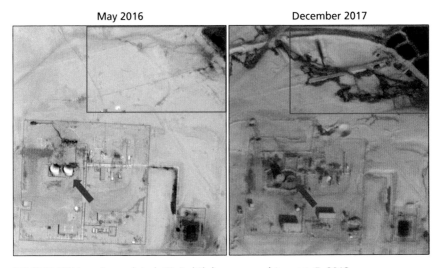

SOURCE: Wikimapia, undated; DigitalGlobe, accessed January 5, 2018.

Water Resources

Given the arid climate of Deir ez-Zor governorate, rehabilitation of water infrastructure after liberation is likely to be a critical need. RAND researchers identified three separate water treatment facilities near Deir ez-Zor city, two in Abu Kamal, and one in Mayadin, as well as a major irrigation pumping station and spillway south of Deir ez-Zor city, the Al Bo-Amr water pumping station.[12] Figure 3.12 shows the primary water treatment facility for drinking water in Deir ez-Zor city. Reports from February 2017 indicated that households in neighborhoods held by the Syrian regime in Deir ez-Zor city did not receive enough water to meet their basic needs.[13] Satellite imagery of this facility shows clearly underutilized treatment tanks and systems on the eastern portion of the facility, suggesting a reduced operational capacity for water filtration in the city. However, neither this facility nor others identified in Mayadin and Abu Kamal showed any signs of major damage from airstrikes.

The Al Bo-Amr facility south of Deir ez-Zor city provided water to irrigate roughly 15,000 acres of irrigated agricultural land along the Euphrates River. News reports from November 2015 suggest that some portions of this facility were damaged, rendering it inoperable.[14] Satellite imagery of this facility, shown in Figure 3.13, confirms that the facility remained offline through 2017—the spillway and downstream channel appeared dry and filled with debris, and the roof of a small building to the south of the spillway was also damaged.

---

[12] Two of the water treatment facilities in Deir ez-Zor city are littoral—one is directly northwest of the Jma'aet El Zohour Quarter of Deir Ez-Zor city, and a second is located downstream along the Euphrates River near Al-Muhasan. A third treatment plant is located to the southeast of the Al-Jorah district of Deir ez-Zor. This is the most likely location of the drinking water treatment plant that distributes water to households. The water pumping station and spillway is located in Al Bo-Amr and provides primary treated water for agriculture but is likely used for domestic water supply as well.

[13] Kerina Tull, *Agriculture in Syria*, K4D Helpdesk Report 133, Brighton, UK: Institute of Development Studies, June 2017.

[14] Christiaan Triebert, "Syria's Bombed Water Infrastructure: An OSINT Inquiry," *Bellingcat*, December 11, 2015.

Figure 3.12
Drinking Water Treatment Plant in Al-Jorah District of Deir ez-Zor City, 2011 and 2017

2011   2017

SOURCE: Imagery from DigitalGlobe, 2017.

Figure 3.13
Al Bo-Amr Pumping Station and Spillway, 2012 and 2017

2012   2017

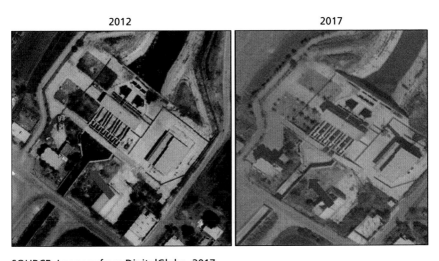

SOURCE: Imagery from DigitalGlobe, 2017.

Internally Displaced Persons

Remote sensing–based estimates of Deir ez-Zor's population suggest that roughly 1.12 million people lived in the governorate as of June 2016.[15] The vast majority of the governorate's inhabitants reside along the Euphrates River Valley (roughly 1 million, or 89 percent). Most of the governorate's major cities (including Deir ez-Zor, Mayadin, and Abu Kamal) rest on the southwest bank of the river. As noted earlier, nearly two-thirds of the governorate's inhabitants live southwest of the Euphrates, while one-third live northeast of the river.

Existing evidence suggests that IDP flows in Deir ez-Zor were relatively modest for most of ISIS's control over the governorate. Remote sensing–based estimates of Deir ez-Zor city's population suggest that the city's population was relatively constant from 2008 to mid-2016.[16] Data on refugee flows from the governorate note that 42,744 individuals were internally displaced in Deir ez-Zor in 2016, and a total of 253,366 were internally displaced in 2017. By way of comparison, Raqqah experienced 65,314 IDPs in 2016 and 491,339 IDPs in 2017, and Aleppo experienced 821,749 and 640,790 IDPs in 2016 and 2017, respectively.[17]

Despite the early pace of refugees from the governorate, the conflict appeared to catch up to Deir ez-Zor at the end of 2017, as SDF and Assad regime forces pushed further and further into the governorate. UN data suggest that as many as 311,000 individuals were displaced in the three months from August 2017 to October 2017 alone, far outpacing other parts of the country.[18]

---

[15] These estimates are derived from Oak Ridge National Laboratory's LandScan data set, which uses census data, NGO reporting, and satellite imagery to estimate the population of each 1-kilometer gridded square on the Earth's surface. For more information, see Egel et al., 2016; Robinson et al., 2017; and Oak Ridge National Laboratory, "LandScan Documentation," undated.

[16] Robinson et al., 2017, p. 154.

[17] UNOCHA, "Syria IDP Flow Data—February 2018," Humanitarian Data Exchange, March 23, 2018b.

[18] UNOCHA, "Syria Crisis: Northeast Syria Situation Report No. 18 (1 October–5 November 2017)," November 2017c.

Recent estimates suggest that roughly 50 percent of IDPs in Deir ez-Zor remained in the governorate. The next-largest contingent (20 percent) traveled northward into Hasakah governorate, followed by 15 percent who have traveled to Raqqah and 11 percent who have traveled to Aleppo.[19] REACH Initiative, 2017b, summarizes these displacement routes.[20]

By late 2017, the two largest IDP camps in Hasakah, Areeshah and al-Hol, could each house approximately 34,000 refugees.[21] UNOCHA cited critical shortages of water and sanitation resources at both camps and overcrowding at the Areeshah facility, which was originally intended as a transit point for refugees traveling further into Syria. Although many tenants at the al-Hol camp have been Iraqi refugees who fled fighting in Mosul, the camp did house roughly 5,500 IDPs from within Syria as of October 2017.[22] Just three months prior, in July 2017, that camp only housed some 600 Syrian IDPs—highlighting the potential for massive growth at this facility in the coming months.[23] Figure 3.14 shows the growth of the al-Hol camp through August 2017. As of January 2018, the size of the al-Hol camp had not appeared to change, and reports of informal IDP camps and settlements in Deir ez-Zor governorate highlighted the dire water and food provision situation.[24] In the ensuing six months, the number of IDP returnees into Deir ez-Zor reportedly climbed up to 198,000 people, although explosive hazard contamination prompted some to flee back into camps in Al-Hasakeh governorate.[25]

---

[19] UNOCHA, October 2017b.

[20] REACH Initiative, "Syria—Deir-ez-Zor Offensive: Overview of Displacement Patterns, Dynamics, and Intentions as Conflict Escalates," September 28, 2017b.

[21] UNOCHA, November 2017c.

[22] UNOCHA, November 2017c.

[23] REACH Initiative, "Syria: REACH Informs on Sectoral Needs of the Over 22,000 Refugees and IDPs Populating al Hol Camp," July 13, 2017a.

[24] UNOCHA, "Syria Crisis: Northeast Syria Situation Report No. 21 (1–31 January 2018)," January 2018a.

[25] UNOCHA, June–July 2018c.

Figure 3.14
Growth in the al-Hol IDP Camp, 2016–2017

SOURCE: Imagery from DigitalGlobe, 2017.
NOTE: The al-Hol IDP camp is located at approximately 36.3759 N, 41.1439 E.

Economic Activity

This section examines local economic activity in Deir ez-Zor, focusing specifically on markets, market prices, and agricultural productivity in the region both under Islamic State control and in recent months.

Market Activity

Prior RAND analysis concluded that throughout 2015 and 2016, markets in ISIS-controlled portions of Deir ez-Zor city were largely empty and inactive. Markets in regime-held areas of the city were much more active, despite being under siege for much of this period.[26] This suggests that the regime was willing to tolerate commerce across front lines with the Islamic State and would likely do so again in the future with SDF-held portions of the larger governorate. Additionally, it suggests that those who are stabilizing cities in Deir ez-Zor may find local markets that have been inactive for some time.

Most market areas in Deir ez-Zor, Mayadin, and Abu Kamal showed few signs of life in visual inspection of recent satellite imagery, as summarized in Figure 3.15. With one exception (in Mayadin), the only active markets in these cities existed in formerly regime-held areas of Deir ez-Zor city.

Figure 3.15
Market Activity in Raqqah and Deir ez-Zor's Major Cities, November 2017

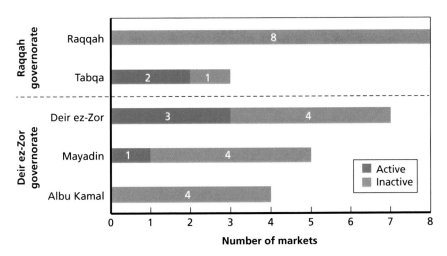

SOURCE: Data from DigitalGlobe imagery, November 2017.

---

[26] Robinson et al., 2017.

Along the less-dense eastern bank of the Euphrates, market and commercial activity in smaller municipalities, such as Abu Hamam, Hajin, and Al Busayrah, also appeared to be largely inactive. Satellite imagery of the main market in Al Busayrah showed normal conditions in May 2017 and some signs of operation until early October 2017, although at a limited capacity. In more recent months, no market activity has been visible, as depicted in Figure 3.16 (right image).

Hajin's city center and commercial and market district showed indications of significant activity as of December 3, 2017 (see Figure 3.17 [left image]). By early January 2018, the market and commercial district appeared empty, with significant damage to the commercial buildings (left side of right image in Figure 3.17). A large berm was also constructed in former agricultural fields, also pictured in Figure 3.17 (right image), likely to fend off liberating forces.[27]

Although it would be challenging to use Raqqah as a baseline for establishing reasonable stabilization benchmarks, it is important

Figure 3.16
Al Busayrah Market, May 2017 and November 2017

May 2017   November 2017

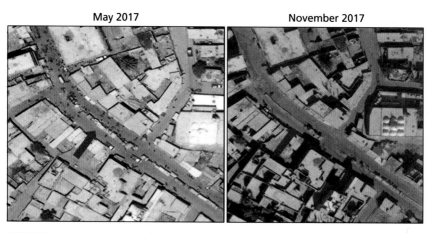

SOURCE: Imagery from DigitalGlobe, 2017.

---

[27] Berms are often used as defensive walls, and its appearance in Hajin's city center in early January 2018 could be the result of local fighting, since SDF began its advance into ISIS-held

Figure 3.17
Hajin City Center, December 2017 and January 2018

December 2017 January 2018

SOURCE: Imagery from DigitalGlobe, 2017.

to note that all eight of the city's market areas appeared shuttered and inactive in imagery from early November 2017.

Tabqa paints a different picture. Prior to the city's full liberation on May 12, 2017, Tabqa's main market area was empty and showed few signs of life. Yet just 36 days later, by June 17, that same market area was bustling, with dozens of market stalls arrayed along a main commercial corridor, significant foot traffic, and hundreds of cars lining the roads. This market is shown in Figure 3.18.

This comparison belies a larger point about the pace with which economic activity returns to cities liberated from the Islamic State. As discussed earlier in this chapter, Raqqah was all but destroyed during the campaign to liberate the city, while damage to Tabqa was considerably more modest. By most estimates, IDP flows from Raqqah accelerated rapidly as SDF forces moved throughout the city, and the presence of explosive remnants of war throughout the city meant that residents were slow to return. While markets in Raqqah remained largely dor-

---

Hajin in late December 2017 (*Syrian War Report*, "Militant Defense Collapses Near Abu Dali," December 29, 2017).

Figure 3.18
Market Activity in Tabqa, June 2017

SOURCE: Imagery from DigitalGlobe, June 17, 2017.

mant, Tabqa sprang back to life. A similar phenomenon occurred in Mosul, where economic activity was quick to resume in East Mosul as civilians returned to their homes but remained largely stagnant in West Mosul, where much of the city was left in ruins.[28]

Phrased differently, economic redevelopment is intrinsically linked to the level of wartime damage and the rate of IDP return after liberation.

Agricultural Activity

Agricultural production in the Deir ez-Zor governorate is characterized by two principal growing seasons: a winter growing season,

---

[28] Jane Arraf, "As East Mosul Comes Back to Life, West Mosul Remains in Ruins," *National Public Radio*, September 28, 2017.

which begins in January and ends in early June, and a summer growing season, which takes place from July to November.[29] During the
winter, barley and wheat are the primary cereal crops produced, and
in summer months, cotton and fruit trees are generally grown. Deir
ez-Zor is a dominant producer of Syria's wheat, barley, and cotton.

All crops grown in Deir ez-Zor require irrigation throughout the
growing season because of the region's highly arid climate and low
rates of precipitation. Wheat, barley, and cotton are water-intensive
crops, with even higher crop water demands in Deir ez-Zor's hot and
arid climate.[30] Deir ez-Zor's agricultural sector has long been particularly vulnerable to any changes in the availability of water because of
climate, overuse, mismanagement or destruction, and damage to irrigation infrastructure.[31] Of note, the UN's FAO reports indicate that
water availability in the Euphrates River, the principal source of water
for agriculture in Deir ez-Zor, has been declining because of upstream
use of water in Turkey. Transboundary water issues have a significant
effect on agricultural productivity in the MERV.

Other key agricultural inputs include seed, fertilizer, pesticide,
insecticide, and fuel. Before 2011, the government provided these
inputs to farmers either without cost or with a significant subsidy.[32]
When such government inputs are not available, farmers will gener-

---

[29] Food and Agriculture Organization (FAO) and World Food Program (WFP), "Special Report—FAO/WFP Crop and Food Security Assessment Mission to the Syrian Arab
Republic," Rome, July 2017.

[30] Cotton, Syria's cash crop, requires near twice the amount of water of wheat and barley.
On average, Deir ez-Zor receives the least amount of precipitation of all governorate in Syria.
Irrigation practices in Deir ez-Zor can be generally categorized as flood irrigation methods,
which require more water to achieve the same crop yield as more water-efficient methods.
Some evidence of movement to more water-efficient methods across the governorate has been
reported by the FAO, but it is likely these efforts have halted because of conflict and lack of
access to government run agricultural loans.

[31] FAO estimates show that average flows in the Euphrates have decreased from a historical
average of 499 cubic meters per second (cms) to 393 cms in more recent years, not accounting
for changes in precipitation. Transboundary water issues will likely receive more attention
during future periods of drought. Also, conflict across Syria has resulted in the widespread
destruction and damage of irrigation canals.

[32] FAO/WFP, 2017.

ally turn to lower-quality and more expensive alternatives that generally decrease agricultural productivity.[33] Transport of farm produce to
markets in conflict-affected areas is problematic due to fuel costs, road
conditions, and limited access to bridges and often results in wastage
and spoilage before arriving at local markets or to collection and storage centers.[34]

Before 2011, Syria's agricultural economy was largely self-suffi-
cient.[35] Syria was considered food-secure, and the agricultural and livestock sector was a source of livelihood for nearly half of the nation's
population.[36] Since 2011, estimates show that the agricultural sector
in Syria has lost nearly $16 billion in food production and damage to
agricultural infrastructure.[37] The erosion of the agricultural sector has
resulted in severe food insecurity and a declining economic base for
much of the nation's farming population.[38] Historically low national
production of wheat and barley occurred during the 2015–2016 grow-

---

[33] For example, seed shortages starting in 2014 caused farmers to begin purchasing seeds
from local markets or using their own retained seed from previous seasons, both of which
have lower germination rates and result in unfavorable variability in crop yield.

[34] Much of agricultural production near Deir ez-Zor city lays on the eastern bank of the
Euphrates River, while major markets like that on Al Wadi Street in the Al Jorah District are
located on the western side of the river.

[35] Carnegie Endowment for International Peace, "Food Insecurity in War-Torn Syria: From
Decades of Self-Sufficiency to Food Dependence," Washington, D.C., June 2015.

[36] Before 2011, livestock production represented 40 percent of all agricultural production
and employed nearly 20 percent of the rural population. Sheep, cattle, and goats made up the
highest percentage of the livestock population, and commercial poultry constituted a large
source of employment. Raising and maintaining livestock requires constant access to feed,
appropriate vaccinations, and the availability of veterinarians. FAO, "Counting the Cost:
Agriculture in Syria After Six Years of Crisis," April 2017.

[37] Nearly 80 percent of households in rural areas still earn their livelihood from crop production, and 26 percent of Syrian gross domestic product was derived from the agricultural
sector in 2016. FAO, 2017.

[38] As of January 2017, public bakeries were in still in operation in Deir ez-Zor city but at
a limited capacity. Humanitarian aid efforts have used airdrops and road deliveries of supplies to prevent malnutrition and starvation, and the World Food Programme also maintains
a series of food supply stocks east of Deir ez-Zor for humanitarian purposes (UNOCHA,
"Syrian Arab Republic: Deir-ez-Zor Flash Update No. 1," January 2017a; Carnegie Endowment for International Peace, June 2015).

ing season, which was attributed to a lack of agricultural inputs, damage to irrigation systems, high costs of fuel and sporadic energy supply, and lack of seeds and fertilizer, as well as civil insecurity and conflict, which impacted access to agricultural fields and access to markets.[39]

In Deir ez-Zor specifically, production losses in the agricultural and livestock sectors resulted in more than $550 million in total losses due to lack of agricultural inputs and general insecurity; $600 million in damages due to livestock death, disease, or theft; and between $250 and $500 million in losses due to destruction of irrigation infrastructure.[40] Existing estimates suggested that rebuilding Deir ez-Zor's agricultural sector could cost as much $1 billion and could require more than $750 million for replenishing livestock.[41]

We plotted historical crop production in Deir ez-Zor governorate in Figure 3.19, using remote sensing data and satellite imagery.[42] This figure compares current levels of production during the 2017 growing season (current case) with average crop production in the years 2009–2016 (average case), and climate-induced contraction in production that occurred during a heavy drought year in 2008 (worst case).

This figure reveals several trends. First, the second growing season for 2016–2017 was largely undetectable in satellite imagery. Even the worst-case scenario (from the 2008 drought) showed higher levels of agricultural productivity. This suggests that the ongoing conflict in Deir ez-Zor either limited access to agricultural fields or restricted

---

[39] FAO/WFP, 2017.

[40] Lack of agricultural inputs is reported as the main constraint on achieving adequate crop yields. Over 70 percent of households in Deir ez-Zor reported that they lacked seeds, and 50 percent reported that they lacked fertilizer. Insecurity is reported as the principal cause of reductions in crop area and the high cost of agricultural inputs. Losses in the livestock sector were particularly high in Deir ez-Zor relative to other governorates (FAO, 2017).

[41] The FAO estimates these values under a "partial return to peace" (FAO, 2017).

[42] Agricultural production is calculated based on a remotely sensed vegetation index, the NDVI, from NASA's moderate resolution imaging spectroradiometer (MODIS) Terra eight-day composite products over land, available at a 250-meter resolution. An NDVI value less than 0.4 generally indicates grassland or sparse vegetation, while higher values indicate agriculture or denser vegetation. MODIS Terra remote sensing data were processed to obtain estimates of NDVI values for agriculture only by applying a discrete global cropland layer to available MODIS Terra data over Syria.

Figure 3.19
Average Seasonal Agricultural Production: Deir ez-Zor (2009–2017)

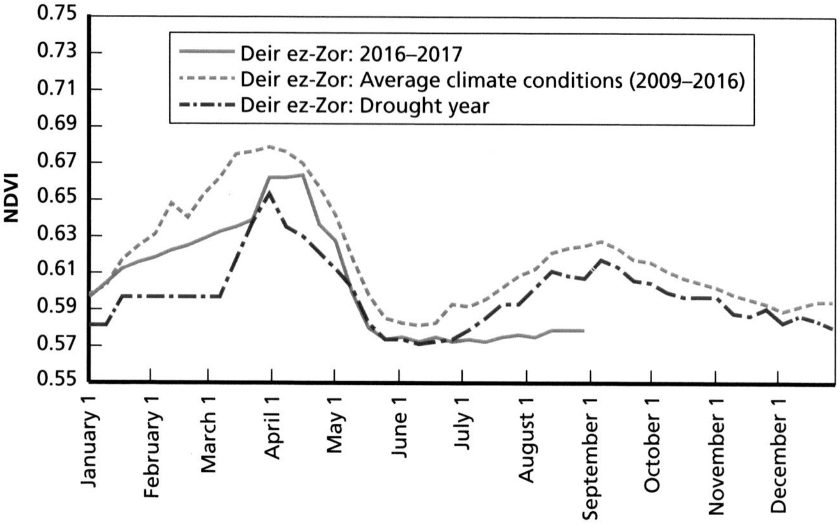

SOURCE: Data from U.S. Department of Agriculture Foreign Agricultural Service, GLAM (Global Agricultural Monitoring) Project, 2017.

flows of necessary inputs. Similar analysis of agricultural productivity in Raqqah and Aleppo governorates (not shown) revealed an identical trend across other conflict-affected areas, suggesting that continuous declines in cultivated areas of wheat and barley since 2011 have taken a toll on overall productivity.[43]

Alternatively, declining productivity in Deir ez-Zor's second growing season was also visible during the 2015–2016 growing season (not shown). This historical trend suggests that scarcity of agricultural inputs may be causing farmers to prioritize the first growing season over the second. Because the second season in this region is typically

---

[43] Total hectares (ha) in production in 2008 for barley were 1,400,000, and in 2017 about 700,000 ha were in production. Total ha in production in 2008 for wheat were 1,500,000, and in 2017 about 1,000,000 ha were in production (FAO/WFP, 2017).

dominated by more-profitable cotton production, this is likely resulting in further deterioration of the economic base for local populations.[44]

This analysis suggests that early stabilization priorities in Deir ez-Zor should focus on providing access to seeds, fertilizers, and affordable fuel before the onset of future growing seasons. Furthermore, efforts to reconstruct wheat and barley storage facilities should be prioritized, to the extent that this will mitigate post-harvest losses and enable any surplus crops to be stored for future use. Longer-term stabilization efforts should encourage the use of more drought-tolerant crops and irrigation systems in the region. While cotton has traditionally served as a cash crop for farmers in Deir ez-Zor, the quantity of water required to cultivate it makes it more vulnerable to shocks. Rebuilding the livestock sector could also help return that industry to the larger portion of the economy it used to represent, but this would require similar longer-term investments in feed, medication, and veterinary care.

Key Findings

The assessment presented in this chapter has revealed a number of findings that should help to prioritize immediate and long-term needs in Deir ez-Zor governorate that stabilization efforts should address.

- **Infrastructure damage** in the governorate appears to be modest compared with other cities liberated from the Islamic State (particularly in Raqqah). Nevertheless, every bridge across the Euphrates River and in the governorate's three main cities was destroyed, and significant damage to industrial facilities has also occurred. Hospitals appear to have been spared the worst of this damage.
- **Electricity** availability in the governorate is minimal at best and rapidly declined over the last year of Islamic State control as military pressure on the governorate increased. Rates of recovery in

---

[44] Cotton is typically exported and viewed across Syria as a cash crop. Cotton is highly water intensive and is likely more difficult to cultivate under limited resources.

other cities liberated from the Islamic State have not been consistent and suggest that recovery should be measured in months, not weeks.

- **Oil and gas resources** are predominantly concentrated on the northeastern side of the Euphrates River, where the SDF has been the primary liberating force. Under ISIS, estimates of the potential value of these resources approach several hundred million dollars a year, and the damage to its production infrastructure appears extensive, as noted above. If SDF-affiliated groups were to retain control of and repair these resources, their main customer is likely to be the Syrian regime itself, based on past behavior under ISIS and the status of key pipeline infrastructure.
- **Water** treatment facilities appeared heavily underutilized or damaged in satellite imagery. Additionally, the main irrigation pumping station in the governorate was damaged and inoperable, likely contributing to major reductions in agricultural productivity.
- **IDP flows** from the governorate radically increased in the final months of 2017, generating greater demands for encampments and relief aid in Hasakah and Raqqa governorates.
- **Markets** across multiple municipalities in the governorate were mostly inactive through early 2018, excluding those in regime-held areas of Deir ez-Zor city. However, evidence from other cities experiencing modest infrastructure damage (mainly Tabqa) suggested that markets may reconstitute quickly after fighting is complete.
- **Agricultural productivity** across the governorate has been declining steadily over the past several years but rapidly worsened over the last growing season in 2017. Upcoming harvests are likely to be the worst in nearly a decade.

To be sure, addressing these needs will not be easy, given that they span regime-controlled and SDF-controlled areas. But, ultimately, stabilization imperatives know no boundaries. Damascus and the SDF may be competitive in many spheres, but they also strongly share a common interest in preventing the reemergence of ISIS. Helping local communities toward stability and longer-term recovery is a critical step toward this goal. Chapter Four will go into detail on the MERV's highly volatile political environment. In Chapter Five, this report will focus on how recovery efforts should be prioritized in that environment.

Navigating the MERV's Geopolitical Complexities

As the previous chapter vividly illustrates, MERV communities have endured a great many hardships in recent years. Well-targeted stabilization efforts may help to alleviate these privations as ISIS is finally pushed out, but those engaged in planning and implementing in this sphere must work though a blend of operational and geopolitical factors in the MERV—factors that will shape how stabilization efforts might be crafted given the confounding realities noted earlier.

On the operational side, geography is a factor. The MERV is an expansive, largely rural venue, and the governorate of Deir ez-Zor through which it flows is very arid. That is not good news for ISIS fighters. There are not too many high-rise buildings in which they can hide or any triple-canopy jungle that would give them cover for launching guerilla attacks.[1] On the other hand, counter-ISIS forces are also facing challenges in terms of regrouping, maneuvering, and engaging across the MERV's wide-ranging terrain. There is also the political reality of distraction—specifically, Turkey's assault on northern Kurdish-held areas in early 2018 that diverted the SDF's attention and operational capacity away from its campaign against ISIS. While the SDF is still a major actor in the MERV, future SDF diversions driven by Ankara's pressures along its border areas with Syria are not

---

[1] As noted by Special Envoy Brett McGurk, ISIS operatives became more vulnerable to targeted attacks by moving into the MERV (U.S. State Department, "Update: Global Coalition to Defeat ISIS," August 4, 2017).

off the table.[2] As a result, clearance operations have not happened in one fell swoop. The campaign to defeat ISIS in the MERV is proving to be a longer, tougher fight.[3] And, as a consequence, stabilization activities are being initiated even as kinetic actions may still be ongoing nearby.

Access into and out of the MERV also poses operational issues. For nongovernment forces and their communities, cross-border access via Turkey is extremely difficult, if not impossible, given Ankara's strong opposition to U.S. support for Kurdish elements in the SDF. Transit routes via northern Iraq have been more accessible but are perilously close to fighting between ISIS and Iraqi Security Forces (ISF), as well as between Kurdish fighters and the ISF in Kirkuk following the Kurdistan region's independence referendum in September 2017. Meanwhile, pro-regime forces in Syria can effectively block access into the valley from southern routes via Jordan, but efforts by Damascus to regain control of the Syrian-Iraq border to the northeast of the MERV would currently require the SDF's active collaboration, which seems unlikely at present.

Geopolitically, a key shaping influence will be the variability of local buy-in for externally supported stabilization. Who can the MERV's Sunni Arab tribes really trust to operate within their domains? Outside the regime's area of control, the SDF has been the most operationally proficient choice for clearing ISIS,[4] but local Sunni Arab communities are not likely to accept the SDF as their "hold" force, given the substantial Kurdish presence in its ranks. The SDF's affiliated Sunni Arab units—broadly arrayed under the SAC—might be more acceptable, but the leadership and operational capacity of these units is uncertain

---

[2]   The SDF's pivot back toward completing its counter-ISIS mission—tagged as Operation Roundup—was launched in early May 2018 (U.S. Central Command, "News Briefing Via Teleconference by U.K. Army Maj. Gen. Felix Gedney, Deputy Commander, Strategy and Support, Combined Joint Task Force–Operation Inherent Resolve," May 8, 2018).

[3]   Per Secretary James Mattis; see U.S. Department of Defense, "Press Gaggle at the Pentagon with Secretary of Defense Mattis," July 27, 2018b.

[4]   A reality for the MERV's tribes is that, given a choice between the Assad regime, ISIS, and the SDF forces, the latter is the least-worst option. View expressed by a Syrian observer, August 8, 2017.

and, as discussed in Chapter Two, the task for forging greater mutual trust within local communities is vulnerable to longstanding frictions among Sunni Arab tribes within the MERV.[5]

And then, of course, there is the Syrian government. After sending reinforcements to free up its forces in Deir ez-Zor city, pro-regime forces swept down the Euphrates' southwest bank, retaking the cities of Mayadin and Abu Kamal. As was illustrated in Figure 1.1, Damascus now controls roughly all habitable areas of Area 3, spanning over 60 percent of the MERV's population. That said, the governorate's extensive oil and gas fields and its upstream water resources are still largely held by Kurdish-led forces.

Given each side's expanding presence in the MERV, is locally focused stabilization really a viable strategy? Clearly, all sides have a stake in sustainably defeating ISIS, and a "bisected" approach to stabilization—with each side working "early recovery" efforts within their respective areas—could offer tangible progress toward that end. Yet, here too, the obstacles are manifold. Damascus has not backed off its insistence on retaking every inch of national territory by force, including areas where the regime hitherto had accepted Russian-orchestrated de-escalation zones. And, internationally, funding for stabilization for Eastern Syria remains whipsawed by geopolitical tensions. Some NATO allies and the European Union have been very reluctant to utilize the counter-ISIS coalition's Syria Recovery Trust Fund, given Turkey's adamant opposition to any funding flows that could aid and abet Kurdish interests. Future U.S. funding for stabilization also remains uncertain, and getting regional partners to follow through on their pledges has been challenging.[6] As for the UN, UN field agencies have gained some access via cross-border convoys, but their cargoes thus far have mainly addressed immediate humanitarian needs (e.g., food, water, shelter), mostly for displaced MERV communities who fled to northern areas.

---

[5]   For a larger discussion, see Kheder Khaddour and Kevin Mazur, *Eastern Expectations: The Changing Dynamics in Syria's Tribal Regions*, The Carnegie Endowment for International Peace, February 2017, pp. 20–22.

[6]   Discussions with U.S. officials, July 2, 2018.

Despite these barriers, and somewhat surprisingly, other factors may influence the parties toward a mutually orchestrated stabilization outcome. To start with, it remains very unclear whether Damascus, even with Russian and Iranian support, really has the military capacity to viably hold Syria's "Western Spine" once all contested areas stretching from Daraa to Idlib and Aleppo governorates are retaken. And while retaking Deir ez-Zor's oil and gas fields is clearly a high priority for the Assad regime, a direct assault against the SDF could pose huge challenges for Damascus, given the extent of northern and eastern Syria that the Kurds currently control, including their traditional homelands. Given these uncertainties, along with their mutual animus toward Ankara, MERV stabilization—while, admittedly, still a hypothetical contingency—could emerge as a key element in a mutually agreed transactional outcome between Damascus and the SDF. The next section addresses the modalities of navigating along this pathway.

Stabilization's Looming Questions

As two rivals in abutting regions attempt to fill the vacuum left by a common enemy's departure, their biggest initial challenge will be to figure out the best ways of relating to each other. The MERV's populated areas have long been interconnected, so behavioral patterns in one part of the valley will impact lives and livelihoods elsewhere. To effectively stabilize the MERV, each side needs to address five key questions.

1. Where Should the Deconfliction Line Be Drawn?

To start with, local implementers and their international partners will need clarity regarding each side's geographical reach. Despite its many twists and turns, the Euphrates River would likely be the easiest choice: It is already mapped, clearly bounded, and easily surveilled. While riverine traffic flows would need to be closely monitored, each side's security forces would be able to police a well-defined, clearly separated boundary line.

But here is the sticking point: The side that has cleared ISIS from a particular venue will likely, and not surprisingly, insist on holding that ground. The Syrian government already has cleared small portions of the river's northeast bank near Deir ez-Zor city, while SDF-affiliated forces may seek to advance west into Abu Kamal's surrounding areas. Consequently, an agreed deconfliction line—as then–Secretary James Mattis once opined—may "look a little more squiggly."[7] And it would likely have to be drawn along back roads, farm fields, hillsides, and surrounding desert areas, not along river banks.

2. Should Cross-Boundary Traffic Be Allowed?

Once each side's geographical presence is clarified, attention will turn to cross-boundary flows of people and goods. As noted earlier, humanitarian relief will have to be delivered to communities in need, and producer-to-vendor supply chains will also need to be reconnected so local markets can recover. An influx of relief aid into the MERV's SDF-controlled areas will most likely come in across the Syrian-Iraqi border, while regime-held areas would be accessed via the transit route from Palmyra. As for local market chains, agricultural producers will want to truck their produce from rural to populated areas, although that would likely flow both ways across the MERV's presumptive deconfliction line.

The key here would be to resurrect the de-escalation concept for Syria that Russia, Turkey, and Iran initially crafted at their conference in Astana, Kazakhstan, in May 2017. If fairly implemented, security zones running "along the lines" of each de-escalation area could be established, along with checkpoints to "ensure the unhindered movement of unarmed civilians and the delivery of humanitarian assistance aid as well as to facilitate economic activities."[8] If this approach were applied in the MERV, the above-cited traffic flows presumably could be channeled through these checkpoints connecting each side's de-

---

[7] Karen DeYoung, "Pentagon Plan to Defeat ISIS Looks Very Much Like Obama's Approach," *Washington Post*, June 28, 2017.

[8] Agreement signed in Astana, Kazakhstan. See Voltaire Network, "Memorandum on the Creation of De-Escalation Areas in the Syrian Arab Republic," May 4, 2017.

escalation area and potentially subject to mutually agreed monitoring presence.[9] The key question here is how to ensure that these checkpoints do not become chokepoints that impede or preclude service delivery, thereby fomenting desperation and hostility in recipient communities. To be sure, there is anecdotal evidence that Syrian truckers have been able to pay for their road access—in effect, transporting commercial goods across contested frontlines of their country's civil war.[10] Yet, under a more formal de-escalation arrangement, it is hard to imagine how such uninterrupted transit would continue if it triggered suspicions of arms trafficking aiding a potentially hostile actor.

3. Can Natural Resources Be Shared?

Third, there is the question of reestablishing access to natural resources. For MERV communities, the most urgent issue is water scarcity, both for direct consumption within its populated areas and for the agricultural irrigation of its farmlands. A large portion of the MERV's upstream watershed is currently under SDF control, including the Tabqa Dam, its associated reservoir (i.e., Lake Assad), and its hydroelectric power stations, all of which ISIS had controlled until the SDF pushed it out in May 2017. But the scarcity problem predates the civil war. The MERV as a whole has long suffered from poorly managed, antiquated irrigation systems, as well as heavy-handed government strictures on farming. The most proximate remedial step would be for Turkey, as the upstream neighbor, to allow a larger flow of water down the Euphrates, per its current international obligations. Ankara's expected quid pro quos would need to be factored into the mix. But, clearly, stabilization over the longer term will require greater water management investments in postwar Syria.[11]

---

[9] Voltaire Network, 2017. Per the agreement, the functioning of these checkpoints and the administration of the zones more generally would be "ensured" by the forces of the three guarantors (e.g., Russia, Turkey, Iran) or by third parties, with the guarantor's consensus.

[10] Discussions with U.S. officials, November 20, 2017.

[11] For background, see Fabrice Balanche, "Water Issues Are Critical to Stability in Syria's Euphrates Valley," *Policy Watch 2622*, Washington Institute for Near East Policy, May 26, 2016.

As for oil generation, the issue is access, not scarcity. As noted earlier, Deir ez-Zor governorate's fields were a huge source of revenue for ISIS, reportedly producing up to 40,000 barrels per day toward the end of 2016. The Islamic State's modus operandi had been to sell crude directly to independent traders who trucked their cargo to mobile refineries or sold it to other traders for cross-border transit.[12] A spike in coalition and Russian air strikes against oil facilities cut overall production and revenues (once in the range of $250–$365 million per year from mostly Syrian sources).[13] These strikes were a key element in degrading ISIS, though they also raised the bar for investments aimed at repairing and restoring petroleum production to prewar levels. No matter who ends up controlling these fields, a viable stabilization strategy would hinge on a revenue-sharing arrangement whereby the resulting revenues could help support the renewal of essential public services on both sides of the larger de-escalation area.

4. How Should Human Displacement Be Managed?

The dynamics of human displacement pose a fourth challenge to stabilization efforts. Since the civil war erupted in 2011, nearly 12 million Syrians have fled their homes, although significant numbers reportedly are now returning to communities largely within areas retaken by Syrian government forces.[14] Within Eastern Syria, the outflow of population was substantial. During 2017, Deir ez-Zor's metropolitan area population was less than half of its prewar levels, where citizens fled regime-opposition violence as well as infighting between ISIS and more moderate opposition groups.[15] As Chapter Three shows, displacement camps, especially in the Raqqah and Hasakah governorates,

---

[12]   Solomon, Kwong, and Bernard, 2016.

[13]   Colin P. Clarke, Kimberly Jackson, Patrick B. Johnston, Eric Robinson, and Howard Shatz, *Financial Futures of the Islamic State of Iraq and the Levant: Findings from a RAND Corporation Workshop*, Santa Monica, Calif.: RAND Corporation, CF-361, 2017, p. 8.

[14]   State Department (2017) cited over 400,000 returnees during 2017. More recent figures are cited in UNOCHA (June–July 2018c).

[15]   USAID, *Syria—Complex Emergency*, Fact Sheet #7, August 4, 2017, noted that just over 90,000 citizens remained compared with its prewar population of over 200,000.

became a prominent feature of the landscape as the counter-ISIS fight ramped up in northeastern Syria.

Liberation's kinetic realities definitely pose issues for stabilization's opening phase. Just as relief providers are already coping with prior displacements, residents in neighborhoods under ISIS control have attempted to flee from the crossfire or from being used as human shields. Inevitably, logistics demands—e.g., for water, food, shelter, and basic medical services—have greatly increased. The flood of outbound noncombatants has stressed screening procedures aimed at preventing the infiltration of ISIS fighters and explosives into IDP camps.[16] The same problem will also apply to returnees, whose influx will generate both humanitarian and security (i.e., "Trojan Horse") concerns. And, finally, as noted earlier, variation in the flows of returnees may also create issues. If stabilization areas are bisected, returnees may be reluctant to go back to regime-held areas even if that is where they once lived. The result may be *in situ* displacement camps, sheltering returnees close to but not inside their communities of origin.

5. Can the Risks of Retributive Violence Be Mitigated?

Finally, perhaps the biggest challenge facing MERV stabilization is the possibility and impacts of targeted violence not just across a de-escalation area but also within its separately held zones. Given that some ISIS fighters will likely seek to blend in and reconstitute themselves, neither side is free from this hazard; but what if, say, Assad regime forces initiate revenge attacks against local communities they perceive to be pro-oppositionist and that they will eventually control? Given the fragile state that postwar Syria will be in, vendettas against non-Islamist opposition forces cold plant the seeds of future conflict.

At their 2017 Astana conference, the Russian, Turkish, and Iranian signatories to the de-escalation agreement were clear that ISIS and jihadi extremists more generally would remain as legitimate targets

---

[16]   Louisa Loveluck and Zakaria Zakaria, "Shocking Conditions Await Civilians Fleeing ISIS in Syria," *Washington Post*, August 19, 2017.

within or around these areas.[17] Preventing a return of ISIS also remains the primary purpose of U.S. forces still operating in Syria. Looking ahead, the question is whether local MERV communities will be singled out and targeted for violent punishment, retribution, or ethnic violence by regime or reconstituted terrorist groups, all of which would undermine postconflict stabilization.

Two Pathways Toward Stabilization

As the foregoing illustrates, any strategy for restoring security and stability in the MERV is going to be hugely challenging to implement. Stabilization is an unavoidable option, to be sure, because any continuation of civil conflict in Eastern Syria will simply refuel local grievances and the resurgence of ISIS—an outcome that no one wants.

How, then, might the Assad regime and nonregime forces proceed? Given their close proximity to each other, amidst ever-present risks of cross-river hostilities (given the absence of a larger peace settlement), as well as attacks by ISIS remnants, stabilization planning will be tightly bounded. Two approaches should receive the greatest scrutiny.

A "Steer Clear" Approach

The first would be a minimalist posture—in essence, a clear division of labor. Each side's policy would be: "You restore security in your area; I'll do so in mine; and we'll just keep our distance from each other." Under this rubric, the Euphrates River would be the buffer. Military deconfliction between U.S. and Russian enabling forces would continue, with restraints also applied to their Syrian partners. Cross-river transit routes would not be restored, and any attempted military movement in this domain would be a targetable violation of deconfliction.

---

[17] Voltaire Network, 2017. The agreement states that parties will "take all necessary measures to continue the fight against DAESH/ISIL" and affiliated groups "as designated by the UN Security Council within or outside the de-escalation areas."

Nonmilitary riverine traffic (e.g., fishing boats) could be allowed subject to overhead surveillance and no cross-river disembarkation.

Clearly, the biggest positive outcome here would be conflict mitigation, assuming that both sides are agreeable. A Euphrates deconfliction line would be comparatively easy to implement. Meanwhile, local civilian councils could be restored; access for relief aid via western and eastern transit corridors would be reopened; and the land-bridge issue could be contained. The downsides, however, are considerable. A continued SDF presence might be necessary for its deterrent value, but that could generate angst among local Sunnis as well as Turkey's adamant opposition. Also, the revival of local markets could be adversely affected if cross-river producer-to-vendor supply chains could not be reestablished. And, finally, returning refugee and IDP families might have to opt for resettlement rather than repatriation to their home communities if they are not able to cross the river.

An "Interactive" Approach

A second, more ambitious strategy would be to rekindle cross-river engagement, albeit in a securely managed and mutually agreed fashion. Under this template, deconfliction efforts would continue, but a larger de-escalation area spanning both sides of the MERV would also be implemented, in effect enabling the cross-river transit (via restored bridging) of unarmed civilians as well as humanitarian relief and economic goods. To assist in this effort, international monitors could be deployed to inspect cross-zonal traffic cargos, and riverine activity could also ramp up, either in accordance with option one, above, or actually crossing the river via mutually agreed points of disembarkation.

On the upside, this interactive approach would definitely help revive local economies via the cross-river flows of people and goods. Producers, vendors, and customers would all benefit. Local governance councils would become more visible with opportunities to engage their counterparts on topics of mutual concern. Meanwhile, returning refugees and IDP families would have a greater choice between heading home or resettling nearby; the presence of international monitors might have a beneficial calming effect; and Iranian ground shipments of military supplies to the Assad regime could be contained or at least deflected by agreed prohibitions on the transiting of weapons through the MERV.

Downsides to this approach include the difficulty of implementing interactive engagements. Ground and riverine transit access could be stymied by the "chokepoint" problem, cited earlier; and while the presence of international monitors might induce a modicum of stability, their presumptively partisan affiliations (e.g., either pro-regime or pro-SDF) might also feed suspicions regarding covert action aimed at undermining their partner's opponents. Also, returning refugees and IDPs might still choose to resettle rather than to repatriate if the security situation is still fragile. And, finally, the SDF's value as a deterrent presence may still feed pressures to keep it in place, albeit with the negative political effects previously noted.

How Best to Proceed?

Looking at the MERV's immediate stabilization needs, there are no perfect options here. Enabling the cross-river influx of humanitarian aid as well as the back and forth movement of people and goods to market will be extremely important for meeting the needs of local communities. And restoring a degree of normalcy to daily life within the MERV would help advance the highest priority for U.S. policy—i.e., denying ISIS fertile ground for reentry—while also keeping the door open for national reconciliation within Syria over the longer term.

That said, given the sociopolitical volatilities and extremist violence that have plagued Eastern Syria in recent years, progress will have to be gradual. Rather than choosing one template over another, both sides could adopt an iterative, incremental way forward—specifically, by starting with the steer clear option and then reassessing whether and how they might shift toward a more ambitious interactive approach. Each will surely be conscious of the other side's strengthens and weaknesses, and their international partners will need to apply constructive leverage—possibly aided by on-the-ground presence—to keep this fragile process moving ahead.

CHAPTER FIVE

Conclusions and Recommendations

As the Islamic State has been pushed out of Eastern Syria's Euphrates Valley, liberated communities are understandably feeling a blend of relief and anxiety. On the one hand, three years of ISIS's tyrannical rule are now behind them. Yet, their future well-being is still very unclear, given deep divisions among Syria's cohort of anti-ISIS actors as well as their international backers. Drawing on the analysis presented in this report's preceding chapters, four overarching conclusions stand out.

Key Conclusions

First, the MERV's early recovery will pivot heavily on restoring basic necessities and access to resources. Alleviating shortfalls of water and electricity, while also ramping up efforts to restore the region's agricultural and petrochemical sectors, should be the highest initial priorities for locally focused stabilization. Getting Deir ez-Zor governorate's oil and gas production facilities back online will be especially valuable, given the sizable revenues they could generate to help fund early recovery. A critical precursor to progress will be the removal of IEDs, booby traps, and landmines that ISIS fighters have likely left behind. While our data sources could not confirm the size and scale of these hazards in the MERV, the experiences of liberating forces and civilian aid providers in Raqqah and Mosul, as well as surrounding rural areas, suggest that unexploded ordnance will pose major access challenges in the MERV.

Second, longer-term recovery efforts will hinge on the quality and character of the MERV's interconnectedness. Given that the MERV's rural domains and major urban centers are located largely on different sides of the Euphrates River, it is unclear how far the agricultural sector can be fully restored if producer-to-vendor supply chains continue to be disrupted by impassable bridges. Repairs of bridging and transportation routes are always high priorities in stabilization venues, but restored access in this case might also feed local angst that the Euphrates River's value as a buffer is being forfeited, given that the larger civil war is still ongoing. Another cloud of uncertainty hangs over the region's displaced populations—specifically, how fast and large the influx of returnees will be, and whether they will choose to repatriate to their home communities or opt for *in situ* displacement in residential areas nearby, given doubts about who is in control of their neighborhoods post-ISIS. The bottom line here is that "bisected" stabilization will have an improvisational quality until cross-MERV access can be safely restored.

Third, stakeholder choices affecting the MERV's post-ISIS stabilization are still very unclear, given Syria's larger volatilities. The two stabilization approaches fleshed out in Chapter Four are best viewed as plausible, albeit hypothetical, contingencies to be orchestrated if—and only if—the SDF and regime forces opt not to forcefully contest the other's presence. For the SDF, uncertainties abound. While it has largely cleared ISIS fighters out of their strongholds, its northward pivot in response to Turkey's recent assaults on Kurdish forces along the Syria-Turkey border will continue to raise questions regarding the SDF's willingness and capacity to complete operations in Eastern Syria as well as to retain control over the region's oil and gas fields.

Damascus is facing its own challenges. Having retaken Eastern Ghouta and Daraa, the Assad regime has ramped up pressures against rebel strongholds in the Idlib governorate. Yet, residual ISIS pockets are still part of the landscape; and, overall, the task of securing Syria's western territory will continue to be a major lift for the regime, likely inhibiting its ability to forcefully retake territory east of the Euphrates River. Also, as noted earlier, Damascus might choose to explore a transactional outcome with the Kurdish-led SDF, offering not to contest the *de facto* autonomy of their Kurdish homeland. Contacts between Damascus and local Syrian Kurdish authorities have already taken place, generating angst in Ankara.[1] The biggest questions here are whether the SDF and the Syrian government could strike a deal on sharing oil and gas revenues and how Kurdish forces would adjust, and possibly downsize, their presence in Deir ez-Zor governorate. In this scenario, the Assad regime could still face pressures to stabilize the governorate, most likely by co-opting the region's more malleable tribal leaders, but how this would play out in practice is very unclear.

Fourth, local buy-in for stabilization will be a critical necessity for ensuring that ISIS does not regain lost ground. On the northeast side of the Valley, given that the SDF does not carry strong legitimacy with local Arab tribes, efforts by the U.S. and partner forces to train, equip, and enable a Sunni Arab hold force will continue to be a vital step in building security capacity that MERV communities would find acceptable. Meanwhile, local civilian councils will also need to work with stakeholders on viable strategies for restoring livelihoods and absorbing the return of displaced communities while also countering violent extremism (CVE) and dealing with explosive hazards. In the CVE sphere, the focus in particular should be on curricular reforms in the educational arena, given ISIS efforts to radicalize youth over the past three years.

As for the Assad regime, it cannot ignore the necessities of achieving a viable pathway toward post-ISIS stabilization. A brutal crackdown by Damascus on Sunni Arab communities in the MERV would simply play to ISIS's advantage, creating fertile ground for its resurgence while also alarming Syria's external patrons who will not want to jump back into the quagmire. As noted above, the regime's strategy may sway toward the cooptation of tribal partners, but even a strategy for playing favorites could not deliver positive results unless there are efforts to address the restoration of a viable economy and livelihoods throughout this fragile region.

---

[1]   Al-Monitor, "Did Israel Nix Russian Deal on Iran-Backed Forces in Syria?" *Week in Review*, July 29, 2018.

Recommended Actions

Given the challenges cited in the previous section, what specific steps should stakeholders take to help set the groundwork for post-ISIS stabilization in the MERV? Geographically, the recommended actions offered here—and ranked in priority order—span the MERV overall, as well as areas northeast of the Euphrates where U.S. support could aid its local coalition partners. Instrumentally, these recommendations also hone in on steps that field practitioners will need to plan for and, subsequently, to orchestrate with the aim of giving on-the-ground stabilization efforts some take-off velocity.

For the MERV Overall

In their early recovery phase, the MERV's communities writ large will be wrestling with an array of immediate and longer-term needs as they adapt to a post-ISIS "new normal." To this end, and recognizing that MERV-wide recovery efforts will inevitably pivot on cooperation from Damascus as well as Syria's neighbors, planners and field practitioners should focus on the following actions:

- **Map out a surge of relief aid that synchronizes wholesale delivery into Eastern Syria with localized distribution at the community level.** Thus far, given the ongoing fight against ISIS, very little in the way of relief assistance has flowed into the MERV. Supplies will need to be trucked into predesignated and secured staging areas where they can be pre-positioned with consignee organizations for local distribution as soon as access is possible.
- **Assess requirements for an expanded network of IDP transit sites and camps.** As noted earlier, there may well be a major influx of returnees in the near future, although uncertainties regarding regime or nonregime presence may affect the scope and direction of repatriation. With Russian assistance, the Syrian government has been especially active in planning for such returns, although the risks remain high for IDPs and refugees returning to their homes, with uncertainty about how they will be received

by the government their legal status, ownership of property, and drafting of males, including boys, into the Syrian armed forces.

- **Ramp up efforts to assist communities in repairing their water treatment facilities, pumping stations, and the electrical grid while also generating short-term agricultural assistance (e.g., seeds, crop storage, and irrigation) for the MERV's next growing season.** The funding sources will vary depending on which side of the Euphrates these investments would be targeted toward, but their link to early recovery is vital.

- **Scope out longer-term plans for reconstituting public services (e.g., public transit, information technology access) and restoring industrial sites.** Local implementation partners, aid organizations, and international donor countries should acknowledge the need for sustained and persistent support for the entire region (and, explicitly, cross-MERV collaboration) to achieve lasting effects.

- **Explore ways to persuade Turkey to allow a larger flow of water down the Euphrates River.** As noted earlier, this would help revive the MERV's agricultural economy while also building greater self-reliance and reducing its reliance on assistance from Kurdish areas. Over the longer term, stabilization efforts in the MERV should also prioritize the use of more drought-tolerant crops and irrigation systems to create added resilience to water shocks.

- **Ensure transparency of international relief aid and external support for local infrastructure repairs.** Greater clarity in these domains would help to assist donor coordination internationally while also providing support for the implementation of cross-MERV transits for interactive stabilization, as sketched out below.

For SDF- and SAC-Held Areas

On the northeast side of the Euphrates, where U.S.-backed partners have expanded their presence, anticipatory steps toward locally focused stabilization should strive for a blend of security and civic assistance efforts even as the fight against ISIS continues. In this domain, planners and field practitioners should focus on the following actions:

- **Generate capacity to assist communities in clearing booby traps, IEDs, car bombs, and unexploded ordnance more generally.** As noted earlier, this is likely a MERV-wide problem, as illustrated by Raqqah's difficult recovery. The SDF and follow-on hold forces will need an expert cohort—probably private-sector implementing partners—to ramp up training for indigenous forces and to undertake direct clearance operations. This is not a mission that humanitarian relief providers are trained or equipped to undertake.
- **Support the formation, operation, and outreach of civil councils at the community level.** Stabilization will ultimately depend on effective oversight by council members over hold force units operating in their geographical space, to include local policing efforts and the responsible management of detention centers where captured ISIS fighters are being held. In addition, efforts to help local councils communicate their activities and intentions and receive feedback from their constituents via social media platforms would be a positive step forward.
- **Ramp up the recruitment, training, and equipping of personnel for SAC's hold force.** Given local anxieties over an extended Kurdish presence in the MERV, this step is an absolute necessity. Initial reports regarding local support for Raqqah's Internal Security Force had been encouraging in terms of the numbers of Sunni Arabs volunteering,[2] but the geographic scope of the MERV's opposition-held areas will generate heightened demands along with some uncertainty regarding the supply of ready and willing recruits.
- **Expand efforts to utilize biometric identity screening as a means for facilitating IDP and refugee returns.** Steps toward expanding sheltering and transit camps, noted above, will assist with repatriation flows, but returnees will likely need to navigate through checkpoints and screening procedures when returning home or transiting to or from markets elsewhere in the valley.

---

[2]   U.S. Department of Defense, "Inherent Resolve Official Briefs Reporters," August 23, 2017b.

- **Develop a fast-track plan for repairing damaged oil pumping and extraction facilities east of the Euphrates, drawing in financial support from regional stakeholders, possibly including Saudi Arabia and the Gulf States.** If the SDF retains control of these facilities, it should have the option for transporting, refining, and selling oil resources outside the Syrian government's system—just as ISIS did—although a revenue-sharing arrangement with Damascus, sketched out below, would be a preferred option and would be vital for implementing any form of stabilization.
- **In the CVE sphere, expand investments to revitalize the education sector's recovery.** This priority will be especially vital, given ISIS efforts to indoctrinate and radicalize youth. Communities will need to focus on curricular reforms, along with expanding access to social media and ensuring funding for the salaries of returning teachers and administrators.

For Implementing Stabilization

Finally, although it remains unclear whether the Syrian government and nonregime forces will opt for a jointly orchestrated stabilization pathway in Eastern Syria, planners and field practitioners do not have the luxury of waiting for clarity. Implementation challenges need to be anticipated and, wherever possible, addressed in advance. To this end, the highest priorities would be the following actions:

- **Map out the MERV's socioeconomic interdependencies, including prospective cross-zonal flows of people and goods.** Such information could guide choices regarding the location and sizing of checkpoints in the interests of reviving the local economy and stabilizing the MERV more generally.
- **Craft a draft joint agreement regarding protocols for processing the transition of cargo and the staff at those checkpoints once cross-zonal transit routes are clarified.** Such an agreement could include international personnel with customs and border protection expertise. Agreements may also be needed for

the clearance and tracking of riverine traffic coming into or exiting the security zone.

- **Develop a plan for how best to allocate revenues generated by hydrocarbon extraction for the purpose of resourcing otherwise underfunded public services (e.g., salaries for teachers and health care providers) on both sides of the MERV.** Those allocations could come either in the form of payments back from Damascus or via a separate carve-out for nonregime-held areas via mobile refineries not under the regime's control.
- **Draft a template that lays out specific and measurable benchmarks for successful stabilization that regime and nonregime actors would aim to achieve within their respective areas of control.** This step would help to set expectations at the community level as well as among international partners regarding the speed and presumptive impacts of early recovery.
- **Anticipate the possibility that stakeholders will need to bring constructive pressures to bear on stabilization implementers aimed at proactively inhibiting targeted violence or vendetta killings.** The keys here would be to jointly identify and track risk-prone situations and make clear the possible costs (i.e., sanctions, loss of access) in situations where security forces on either side choose to inflict heavy-handed crackdowns that simply play into the hands of jihadi extremists.

To be sure, these recommended actions cannot speak to all of the looming challenges that stabilization efforts might face in navigating across the MERV's exceedingly complex terrain. But these interlinked steps do flag some of the highest-priority actions that stakeholders should consider as part of larger efforts to press ahead on collaboratively and sustainably defeating ISIS while also ultimately moving toward a larger peace settlement aimed at bringing Syria's tragic civil war to closure.

References

Al-Hayat, "Najun Yarawun lil Marra al-Uwla Waqa'a' Qatl 800 fi Majzarat 'Ashirat al-Shaytat" ("The Saved See for the First Time the Evidence of the Killing of 800 in the Massacre of the Shaytat Tribe"), October 3, 2014.

Al-Monitor, "Did Israel Nix Russian Deal on Iran-Backed Forces in Syria?" *Week in Review*, July 29, 2018. As of October 16, 2018:
http://www.al-monitor.com/pulse/originals/2018/07/
israel-nix-russia-deal-iran-backed-forces-syria.html#ixzz5Nnm9ju3L

Arraf, Jane, "As East Mosul Comes Back to Life, West Mosul Remains in Ruins," *National Public Radio*, September 28, 2017. As of November 21, 2017:
https://www.npr.org/sections/parallels/2017/09/18/551482635/
as-east-mosul-comes-back-to-life-west-mosul-remains-in-ruins

Asharq al-Awsat, "Kharitat al Milishiat al-Iraniya fi Suriya" ("The Map of Iranian Militias in Syria"), August 23, 2017.

Balanche, Fabrice, "Water Issues Are Critical to Stability in Syria's Euphrates Valley," *Policy Watch 2622*, Washington Institute for Near East Policy, May 26, 2016. As of November 21, 2017:
http://www.washingtoninstitute.org/policy-analysis/view/
water-issues-are-crucial-to-stability-in-syrias-euphrates-valley

Barnard, Anne, and Hwaida Saad, "To Freeze Syria War, Russia Proposes Setting up 'De-Escalation Zones,'" *New York Times*, May 3, 2017. As of November 21, 2017:
https://www.nytimes.com/2017/05/03/world/middleeast/
russia-syria-de-escalation-zones-astana.html

Batatu, Hanna, *Syria's Peasantry, the Descendants of Its Less Rural Notables, and Their Politics*, Princeton, N.J.: Princeton University Press, 1999.

Carnegie Endowment for International Peace, "Food Insecurity in War-Torn Syria: From Decades of Self-Sufficiency to Food Dependence," Washington, D.C., June 2015. As of November 21, 2017:
http://carnegieendowment.org/2015/06/04/food-insecurity-in-war-torn-syria-from-decades-of-self-sufficiency-to-food-dependence-pub-60320

Chatty, Dawn, "Al-Qaba'il wa al-Qabaliya wa al-Hawiya al-Siyasiya fi Suriya al-Mu'asira" ("The Tribes, Tribalism, and Political Identity in Contemporary Syria"), *Omran Journal for Sociology and Anthropology*, Vol. 4, No. 15, January 2016, pp. 81–96.

Clarke, Colin P., Kimberly Jackson, Patrick B. Johnston, Eric Robinson, and Howard Shatz, *Financial Futures of the Islamic State of Iraq and the Levant: Findings from a RAND Corporation Workshop*, Santa Monica, Calif.: RAND Corporation, CF-361, 2017. As of November 21, 2017:
http://www.rand.org/pubs/conf_proceedings/CF361.html

Culbertson, Shelly, and Linda Robinson, *Making Victory Count After Defeating ISIS: Stabilization Challenges in Mosul and Beyond*, Santa Monica, Calif.: RAND Corporation, RR-2076-RC, 2017. As of November 21, 2017:
https://www.rand.org/pubs/research_reports/RR2076.html

Davis, Julie Hirschfeld, "Trump Drops Push for Immediate Withdrawal of Troops from Syria," *New York Times*, April 4, 2018. As of November 14, 2018:
https://mobile.nytimes.com/2018/04/04/world/middleeast/trump-syria-troops.html

DeYoung, Karen, "Pentagon Plan to Defeat ISIS Looks Very Much Like Obama's Approach," *Washington Post*, June 28, 2017. As of November 21, 2017:
https://www.washingtonpost.com/world/national-security/pentagon-plan-to-defeat-isis-looks-very-much-like-obamas-approach/2017/06/28/d43aa1b6-5c30-11e7-a9f6-7c3296387341_story.html

DigitalGlobe, "DigitalGlobe Cloud Services," undated. As of November 21, 2017:
https://services.digitalglobe.com/

Egel, Daniel, Charles P. Ries, Ben Connable, Todd Helmus, Eric Robinson, Isaac Baruffi, Melissa A. Bradley, Kurt Card, Kathleen Loa, Sean Mann, Fernando Sedano, Stephan B. Seabrook, and Robert Stewart, *Investing in the Fight: Assessing the Use of the Commander's Emergency Response Program in Afghanistan*, Santa Monica, Calif.: RAND Corporation, RR-1508-OSD, 2016. As of November 21, 2017:
http://www.rand.org/pubs/research_reports/RR1508.html

FAO—*See* United Nations Food and Agriculture Organization.

FAO and WFP—*See* United Nations Food and Agriculture Organization and World Food Programme.

Faucon, Benoit, and Margaret Coker, "The Rise and Deadly Fall of Islamic State's Oil Tycoon," *Wall Street Journal,* April 24, 2016. As of November 21, 2017: https://www.wsj.com/articles/ the-rise-and-deadly-fall-of-islamic-states-oil-tycoon-1461522313

Heras, Nicholas, Bassam Barabandi, and Nidal Betare, *Deir Azzour Tribal Mapping Project*, Washington, D.C.: Center for a New American Security, September 2017.

Heras, Nicholas, and Omar Abu Layla, "The Security Vacuum in Post-ISIS Deir Ezzor," *Syria Deeply*, November 15, 2017.

Hoover Institution, "Secretary of State Rex W. Tillerson Discusses 'The Way Forward in Syria' with Condoleezza Rice," Stanford, Calif.: Stanford University, January 17, 2018. As of November 14, 2018: https://www.hoover.org/events/tillerson_11718

Khaddour, Kheder, and Kevin Mazur, *Eastern Expectations: The Changing Dynamics in Syria's Tribal Regions*, Carnegie Endowment for International Peace, February 2017. As of November 2017: http://carnegie-mec.org/2017/02/28/ eastern-expectations-changing-dynamics-in-syria-s-tribal-regions-pub-68008

Loveluck, Louisa, and Zakaria Zakaria, "Shocking Conditions Await Civilians Fleeing ISIS in Syria," *Washington Post*, August 19, 2017. As of November 21, 2017: https://www.washingtonpost.com/world/middle_east/ shocking-conditions-await-civilians-fleeing-isis-in-syria/2017/08/18/ c5d7e9c6-841c-11e7-9e7a-20fa8d7a0db6_story.html

Micro Syria, "Nahwa Mazid min al-'Askara: Al-Liwa'Abu Muhannad Samra Muhafizhan lama Tabqa min Deir Ezzour" ("Towards Additional Militarization: General Abu Muhannad Is the Governor of What Remains of Deir Ezzour"), October 27, 2016

National Oceanic and Atmospheric Administration, "Version 1 VIIRS Day/Night Band Nighttime Lights," undated. As of November 21, 2017: https://ngdc.noaa.gov/eog/viirs/download_dnb_composites.html

NOAA—*See* National Oceanic and Atmospheric Administration.

Oak Ridge National Laboratory, "LandScan Documentation," undated. As of March 10, 2017: http://web.ornl.gov/sci/landscan/landscan_documentation.shtml

Operation Inherent Resolve, "Operation Inherent Resolve Update Brief with Maj. Gen. Gedney," December 27, 2017. As of November 14, 2018: http://www.inherentresolve.mil/Video/videoid/577434/dvpsearch/gedney/dvpcc/ false/#DVIDSVideoPlayer2329

Orient Research Centre, "Sharqi Suriya bayn Qasd wa al-Assad" ("Eastern Syria Between the SDF and Assad"), undated.

REACH Initiative, "Syria: REACH Informs on Sectoral Needs of the Over 22,000 Refugees and IDPs Populating Al Hol Camp," July 13, 2017a. As of November 21, 2017:
http://www.reach-initiative.org/
syria-reach-informs-on-sectoral-needs-of-the-over-22000-refugees-and-idps-populating-al-hol-camp

REACH Initiative, "Syria—Deir-ez-Zor Offensive: Overview of Displacement Patterns, Dynamics, and Intentions as Conflict Escalates," September 28, 2017b. As of October 16, 2018:
http://www.reach-initiative.org/
deir-ez-zor-offensive-overview-of-displacement-patterns-dynamics-and-intentions-as-conflict-escalates

Robinson, Eric, Daniel Egel, Patrick B. Johnston, Sean Mann, Alexander D. Rothenberg, and David Stebbins, *When the Islamic State Comes to Town: The Economic Impact of Islamic State Governance in Iraq and Syria*, Santa Monica, Calif.: RAND Corporation, RR-1970-RC, 2017. As of November 21, 2017:
https://www.rand.org/pubs/research_reports/RR1970.html

RT Arabic News, "Muhafizh Deir Ez Zour Yuhadid Takalif I'adat Bina' al-Madina" ("The Governor of Deir Ezzour Determines the Cost of the City's Reconstruction"), November 8, 2017.

Sands, Phil, "Oil, Food and Protest in Syria's Restive East," *The National,* January 17, 2012. As of March 10, 2017:
http://www.thenational.ae/news/world/middle-east/
oil-food-and-protest-in-syrias-restive-east

Sharma, Suraj, "Turkey Sends Power Lines into Syrian Town Cleared of IS," *Middle East Eye,* September 8, 2016. As of November 21, 2017:
http://www.middleeasteye.net/news/
turkey-sends-power-lines-syrian-town-cleared-21416447

Solomon, Erika, Robin Kwong, and Steven Bernard, "Inside ISIS Inc: The Journey of a Barrel of Oil," *Financial Times,* February 29, 2016. As of November 21, 2017:
http://ig.ft.com/sites/2015/isis-oil/

Solomon, Erika, and Ahmed Mhidi, "ISIS Inc: Syria's 'Mafia-Style' Gas Deals with Jihadis," *Financial Times,* October 15, 2015. As of November 21, 2017:
https://www.ft.com/content/92f4e036-6b69-11e5-aca9-d87542bf8673

Syrian War Report, "Militant Defense Collapses Near Abu Dali," December 29, 2017. As of November 14, 2018:
https://southfront.org/
syrian-war-report-december-29-2017-militant-defense-collapses-near-abu-dali/

Torbati, Yeganeh, "Islamic State Yearly Oil Revenue Halved to $250 Million: U.S. Official," Reuters, May 11, 2016. As of November 21, 2017:
http://www.reuters.com/article/
us-mideast-crisis-islamic-state-revenue-idUSKCN0Y22CW

Triebert, Christiaan, "Syria's Bombed Water Infrastructure: An OSINT Inquiry," *Bellingcat*, December 11, 2015. As of November 21, 2017:
https://www.bellingcat.com/news/mena/2015/12/11/
syrias-bombed-water-infrastructure/

Tull, Kerina, *Agriculture in Syria*, K4D Helpdesk Report 133, Brighton, UK: Institute of Development Studies, June 2017. As of November 21, 2017:
https://opendocs.ids.ac.uk/opendocs/handle/123456789/13081

U.S. Agency for International Development, "Syria Complex Emergency—Fact Sheet #7," August 4, 2017. As of November 21, 2017:
https://www.usaid.gov/crisis/syria/fy17/fs07

U.S. Central Command, "News Briefing Via Teleconference by U.K. Army Maj. Gen. Felix Gedney, Deputy Commander, Strategy and Support, Combined Joint Task Force–Operation Inherent Resolve," May 8, 2018. As of November 14, 2018:
http://www.centcom.mil/MEDIA/Transcripts/Article/1522075/
news-briefing-via-teleconference-by-uk-army-maj-gen-felix-gedney-deputy-
command/

U.S. Department of Agriculture Foreign Agricultural Service, GLAM (Global Agricultural Monitoring) Project, 2017. As of May 19, 2018:
https://ipad.fas.usda.gov/glam.htm

U.S. Department of Defense, "Department of Defense Press Briefing by Colonel Dillon via Teleconference from Baghdad, Iraq," August 3, 2017a. As of November 21, 2017:
https://www.defense.gov/News/Transcripts/Transcript-View/Article/1267146/
department-of-defense-press-briefing-by-colonel-dillon-via-teleconference-from/

U.S. Department of Defense, "Inherent Resolve Official Briefs Reporters," August 23, 2017b. As of November 21, 2017:
https://www.defense.gov/Videos/videoid/545316/#DVIDSVideoPlayer1133

U.S. Department of Defense, "Department of Defense Press Briefing by Pentagon Chief Spokesperson Dana W. White and Joint Staff Director Lt. Gen. Kenneth F. McKenzie Jr. in the Pentagon Briefing Room," March 15, 2018a. As of November 14, 2018:
https://www.defense.gov/News/Transcripts/Transcript-View/Article/1467771/
department-of-defense-press-briefing-by-pentagon-chief-spokesperson-dana-w-
whit/

U.S. Department of Defense, "Press Gaggle at the Pentagon with Secretary of Defense Mattis," July 27, 2018b. As of November 14, 2018:
https://www.defense.gov/News/Transcripts/Transcript-View/Article/1586807/press-gaggle-at-the-pentagon-with-secretary-of-defense-mattis/

U.S. Department of State, "Remarks at a Press Availability," August 1, 2017a. As of November 21, 2017:
https://www.state.gov/secretary/20172018tillerson/remarks/2017/08/272979.htm

U.S. Department of State, "Update: Global Coalition to Defeat ISIS," August 4, 2017b. As of November 21, 2017:
https://www.state.gov/r/pa/prs/ps/2017/08/273198.htm

U.S. Department of State, "Joint Statement by the President of the United States and the President of the Russian Federation," November 11, 2017c. As of November 21, 2017:
https://www.state.gov/r/pa/prs/ps/2017/11/275459.htm

U.S. Energy Information Administration, "Syria Selected Energy Infrastructure," undated. As of November 21, 2017:
https://www.eia.gov/beta/international/analysis_includes/countries_long/Syria/images/syria_map.png

U.S. Institute of Peace, "Iraq and Syria: Views from the U.S. Administration, Military Leaders and the Region," panel discussion, Washington, D.C., April 3, 2018. As of November 14, 2018:
https://www.usip.org/events/iraq-and-syria-views-us-administration-military-leaders-and-region

U.S. Institute of Peace and the U.S. Army War College, Peacekeeping and Stability Operations Institute, *Guiding Principles for Stabilization and Reconstruction*, Washington, D.C.: USIP Press, 2009. As of November 14, 2018:
https://www.usip.org/sites/default/files/guiding_principles_full.pdf

United Nations Food and Agriculture Organization, "Counting the Cost: Agriculture in Syria After Six Years of Crisis," April 2017. As of November 21, 2017:
http://www.fao.org/emergencies/resources/documents/resources-detail/en/c/878213/

United Nations Food and Agriculture Organization and World Food Programme, "Special Report—FAO/WFP Crop and Food Security Assessment Mission to the Syrian Arab Republic," Rome, July 2017. As of November 21, 2017:
https://reliefweb.int/report/syrian-arab-republic/special-report-faowfp-crop-and-food-security-assessment-mission-syrian-1

United Nations Office of the Coordinator for Humanitarian Assistance, "Syrian Arab Republic: Deir-ez-Zor Flash Update No. 1," January 2017a. As of November 21, 2017:
https://reliefweb.int/report/syrian-arab-republic/
syria-arab-republic-deir-ez-zor-flash-update-no-1-20-january-2017-enar

United Nations Office of the Coordinator for Humanitarian Assistance, "Syria IDP Flow Data—September 2017," Humanitarian Data Exchange, October 23, 2017b. As of November 21, 2017:
https://data.humdata.org/dataset/september-2017-idp-flow-data

United Nations Office of the Coordinator for Humanitarian Assistance, "Syria Crisis: Northeast Syria Situation Report No. 18 (1 October–5 November 2017)," November 2017c. As of November 21, 2017:
https://reliefweb.int/sites/reliefweb.int/files/resources/
NES%20Sit%20Rep%20October%20monthly%20no%2018%20draft%20
FINAL.pdf

United Nations Office of the Coordinator for Humanitarian Assistance, "Syria Crisis: Northeast Syria Situation Report No. 21 (1–31 January 2018)," January 2018a. As of November 14, 2018:
https://reliefweb.int/sites/reliefweb.int/files/resources/
Humanitarian%20response%20NES%20Jan2018_2.pdf

United Nations Office of the Coordinator for Humanitarian Assistance, "Syria IDP Flow Data—February 2018," Humanitarian Data Exchange, March 23, 2018b.

United Nations Office of the Coordinator for Humanitarian Assistance, "Syria Crisis: Northeast Syria Situation Report No. 26 (15 June–15 July 2018)," July 2018c. As of October 16, 2018:
https://www.humanitarianresponse.info/sites/www.humanitarianresponse.info/
files/documents/files/north_east_syria_sit_rep_15_june_to_15_july.pdf

UNOCHA—*See* United Nations Office of the Coordinator for Humanitarian Assistance.

Voltaire Network, "Memorandum on the Creation of De-Escalation Areas in the Syrian Arab Republic," May 4, 2017. As of November 21, 2017:
http://www.voltairenet.org/article196287.html

Wikimapia, "Wikimapia," undated. As of November 21, 2017:
http://wikimapia.org/#lang=en&lat=35.930000&lon=39.020000&z=8